T0360728

An excellent and powerful book, which is of pivotal interest for all students, researchers, academics and practitioners on an international scale. The ideas are novel, thought provoking and the material makes scholars re-address issues, and realign our thoughts to new thematic areas and possibilities in our field.

—Ritsa Ventouratos-Fotinatos, *Professor Organisational Psychology, The American College of Greece*

Work and Stress

Stress is a leading cause of ill health in the workplace. This shortform book analyses, summarizes and contextualizes research around stress at work.

The book begins by exploring the impact and challenges of technology and the challenging and changing contours and boundaries of the nature of work. Using a behaviour lens, the authors draw on cyberpsychology to illuminate the choices we make to balance life, work and well-being. The changing nature of work is analysed, shifting structures and boundaries explored and the stress consequences of such themes as the Gig economy and precarious work are also included in the book.

A compelling framework for researchers of work, organization and psychology, this concise book is also valuable reading for reflective practitioners, seeking to understand the importance of well-being in the workplace.

Philip Dewe is an Emeritus Professor at Birkbeck, University of London. He has written widely on work stress research and coping. He is a Fellow of the Academy of Social Sciences, the European Academy of Occupational Health Psychology and Birkbeck, University of London.

Cary L. Cooper, CBE, is the 50th Anniversary Professor of Organizational Psychology and Health at the ALLIANCE Manchester Business School, University of Manchester; President of the CIPD and Chair of the National Forum for Health and Wellbeing at Work.

State of the Art in Business Research
Series Editor: Geoffrey Wood

Recent advances in theory, methods and applied knowledge (alongside structural changes in the global economic ecosystem) have presented researchers with challenges in seeking to stay abreast of their fields and navigate new scholarly terrains.

State of the Art in Business Research presents shortform books which provide an expert map to guide readers through new and rapidly evolving areas of research. Each title will provide an overview of the area, a guide to the key literature and theories and time-saving summaries of how theory interacts with practice.

As a collection, these books provide a library of theoretical and conceptual insights, and exposure to novel research tools and applied knowledge, that aid and facilitate in defining the state of the art, as a foundation stone for a new generation of research.

Management and Organizational History
A Research Overview
Albert J. Mills and Milorad M. Novicevic

Employee Engagement
A Research Overview
Brad Shuck

Operations Management
A Research Overview
Michael A. Lewis

Work and Stress
A Research Overview
Philip Dewe and Cary L. Cooper

Work and Stress

A Research Overview

Philip Dewe and
Cary L. Cooper

Routledge
Taylor & Francis Group

LONDON AND NEW YORK

First published 2021
by Routledge
2 Park Square, Milton Park, Abingdon, Oxon OX14 4RN

and by Routledge
52 Vanderbilt Avenue, New York, NY 10017

Routledge is an imprint of the Taylor & Francis Group, an informa business

© 2021 Philip Dewe and Cary L. Cooper

The right of Philip Dewe and Cary L. Cooper to be identified as authors of this work has been asserted by them in accordance with sections 77 and 78 of the Copyright, Designs and Patents Act 1988.

British Library Cataloguing-in-Publication Data
A catalogue record for this book is available from the British Library

Library of Congress Cataloging-in-Publication Data
A catalog record has been requested for this book

ISBN: 978-0-367-34756-7 (hbk)
ISBN: 978-0-429-33101-5 (ebk)

Typeset in Times New Roman
by Wearset Ltd, Boldon, Tyne and Wear

Contents

Chapter 1

Organizational psychology, organizational behaviour and workplace stress

We begin this book by reflecting on alternative approaches and movements that have, since the beginning of this millennium, shaped organizational psychology and organizational behaviour, and set researchers with a responsibility to be mindful and to question what this means for workplace stress research. These developments spawned by economic crisis and turbulence, the ever present and always ready portable technologies, and the tsunami of globalization (Dewe & Cooper 2017) define the context of stress research. It is this context which shapes our research, gives it explanatory power, and sets the challenges for the direction and the relevance of what we do. These alternative approaches and movements acknowledge this context and, indeed, have significantly shaped our understanding and the state of our knowledge, and influenced the nature of our discipline; testing our ability as researchers to 'achieve a more meaningful integration of findings across the array of topics researched' (Porter & Schneider 2014, p. 15).

The 'good news', as Cooper (2009, p. 7) points out, is 'that organizational behaviour [and organizational psychology] moves with the times, and reflects the issues, concerns and dilemmas of the age and beyond'. Nevertheless, these new pathways and new developments, coupled with the speed at which the context changes, its reach and authority, 'calls for the refining of existing theories, methods and practice' (Dewe & Cooper 2017, p. 93). It is a powerful reminder for us to recognize and, at times, question not just where our theories are taking us, but also how well they express the realities of the workplace. Giving power and legitimacy to concepts like context, relevance, refinement and, of course, our moral responsibilities to those whose working lives we research (Dewe & Cooper 2017). Taken together these concepts provide a platform and a foundation for building and developing our research into workplace stress, giving it meaning and balance.

Alternative approaches and movements

We begin by pointing to the movements that have shaped our discipline, turning first to exploring the scope and reach of what has become known as the *positive psychology movement* (Seligman & Csikszentmihalyi 2000). Positive psychology 'has experienced extraordinary growth in the past decade' elevating it to the status of a 'popular culture movement' (Hart & Sasso 2011, pp. 82; 88). Recently researchers have 'taken stock' and explored 'trends' in this movement, suggesting that its boundaries are changing and 'a new identity is emerging for positive psychology in the second decade of the millennium' (Hart & Sasso 2011, pp. 82; 91). What has been described as 'positive psychology 2.0' offers a balanced approach that will 'pay more attention to' both 'the positive and negative', and so the need now is 'to enhance the positives and manage the negatives in order to increase well-being and decrease mental illness' moving 'the focus away from individual happiness and success to a meaning-centred approach to making life better for all people'. This approach 'depicts the complex interactions in living a full life ... and embrace[s] life in totality' – the good and the bad (Wong 2011, pp. 69; 77).

'Following the lead of positive psychology' saw the arrival in the workplace of the field of *Positive Organizational Behavior* (POB) (Youssef & Luthans 2007, p. 774) and *Positive Organizational Scholarship* (Cameron, Dutton & Quinn 2003). There is now, argues Youssef and Luthans, 'an attempt to study new, or at least relatively unique to the workplace positive psychological resource capacities' (2007, p. 775). Similarly, positive organizational scholarship offers a lens through which to examine 'new or different mechanisms through which organizational dynamics and positive organizational processes produce extraordinary positive or unexpected outcomes' (Cameron *et al.*, 2003, p. 6). Both are oriented to investigating 'human resource strengths and psychological capacities that can be measured, developed, and effectively managed' (Youssef & Luthans 2007, p. 775). Building on a growing literature, POB's four 'criteria-meeting capacities' selected for examination results in what the authors (Luthans, Youssef & Avolio 2007) call *psychological capital* ('self-efficacy, optimism, hope, and resiliency'), 'that operate additively but also perhaps, synergistically' (p. 19). They, focus on the development of 'positive psychological resource capacities', ushering in new challenges for researchers to explore new programmes, new opportunities to examine other positive constructs (e.g. 'creativity and wisdom').

Not forgetting the development of new innovations around training interventions that all reflect this new positive perspective, which offers a new era in workplace research and potential positive interventions (Luthans *et al.*, 2007, p. 18).

Other changes are afoot. The dynamics of this changing context has brought innovation, creativity, new opportunities, and paradigms that shift the boundaries of organizational psychology and the focus of its investigations and research. Many of these changes are built around the 'need to effectively adapt to changes, [as it] affects all people and all organizations', offering to organizational psychology the opportunity to establish 'a new mandate, helping individuals and organizations adjust to rapidly changing conditions' (Muchinsky 2006, p. 23). These developments include the growing interest in well-being through the lens of *human capital*. As mentioned above, there is psychology capital (Luthans *et al.*, 2007). But the ideas surrounding human capital now reflects a rich, and growing literature that covers: (i) intellectual capital (Roslender 2009; Roslender 2009a) – accounting for people – focuses on employees as 'a crucial source of value' for organizations, and 'a resource that requires careful management, if it is to fulfil its maximum potential' (Roslender & Fincham 2001, p. 383), (ii) hedonic capital (Graham & Oswald 2010) – 'stocks of psychological resources available to an individual' and 'how it produces well-being' (pp. 373; 374), and (iii) the 'new human capital equation' – 'human capital and its contribution to business' (Cascio 2007, p. 15). In addition, (iv) resource-based strategies – competing through people (Dewe & Cooper 2017, p. 15). Then there has been a call for the development of a *psychology of older workers*, as distinct from a psychology of ageing, drawing attention to the 'age wave' (Macik-Frey, Quick & Nelson 2007, p. 830) to capture the motivations and aspirations of older workers.

Then there is the need 'to acknowledge the importance' of *occupational health psychology* (Dewe & Cooper 2017, p. 91), bringing a perspective that investigates the need 'to promote and protect' the quality of working life and the health and well-being of workers (Barling & Griffiths 2003, p. 30; Dewe & Cooper 2017, pp. 90–91). In order to broaden its focus 'we might modify the concept of occupational health psychology to **organizational health psychology**' as it then offers an approach that 'help[s] individuals and organizations (of all types) adapt to rapid and unrelenting change' (Muchinsky 2006, p. 23). Not forgetting that we are 'in the midst of an *[affective] revolution*' (Barsade, Brief & Spataro 2003, p. 33), one that 'was slow in coming even though the need for more research to understand this "missing ingredient" of organizational life has long been acknowledge' (Dewe & Cooper 2017, p. 73; Fineman 2004, p. 720). The notion of 'emotions at work' has also found its place in work stress research, with the dictum from the work by Lazarus & Cohen-Charash (2001, p. 45) that 'discrete emotions are the "coin of the realm" when exploring the coping process'.

Another entry shaping our discipline is the work surrounding 'cyberpsychology' (Dewe & Cooper 2017, p. 5). From a fast-growing literature, researchers have explored behaviours and concepts like 'technostress' (Tarafdar, Tu & Ragu-Nathan 2010), 'problematic inter-net use' (Chiang & Su 2012), 'dependency and addiction' (Griffiths 1995; 2010), 'cyberslacking and cyberloafing' (Lim & Chen 2012), and 'cyberbullying' (Sabella, Patchin & Hinduja 2013). While the term technostress was offered by Brod in 1982, this work has 'found its voice and established its place in work stress research in the new mil-lennium' (Dewe & Cooper 2017, p. 121). We are 'in a work environ-ment that is now even more technologically and socially wired than ever before' (Barjis, Gupta & Sharda 2011, p. 615). Now, with researchers emphasizing the 'fourth dimensional' nature of our world, our belief is the scope of work stress research should be broadened beyond technostress to capture the impact on our behaviours of this mobile 'digital everywhereness' (Scott 2016, p. 17). What Shadbolt and Hampson describe as 'our hyper-complex environment' (2018, p. 22). Technology is also reshaping *leadership* research. Here, Schwab argues, describing advances in technology as the 'fourth industrial revolution' 'then this will demand a new type of leadership – systems leadership – [where] leadership will be needed on how these advances 'are governed and the values they exhibit 'in the way they affect' people, organizations and communities' (2018b, pp. 14–16; 220). Leadership research has also found itself, in this millennium, called to consider the issue of – 'the confidence of the incompetent' (Fritz 2019, p. 1/35; Kruger & Dunning 1999; Staub & Kaynak 2014).

A shift in focus to those forces shaping workplaces, we explore the globalization of the interest in well-being and the impact of this interest on the measuring of GNP, suggesting that GNP measurement needs to focus more on 'social progression' (OECD 2012, p. 2). Associated with this interest is the idea that GNP measurement should better express the 'quality of life'. The OECD report (2009) suggests that 'measures of subjective well-being provide key information about people's "quality of life" and that statistical offices should incorporate questions to capture people's life evaluations, hedonic experiences and priorities in their own surveys' (Stiglitz, Sen & Fitoussi 2009, p. 58). With a significant movement towards expanding the scope of measuring GNP, a growing interest has also emerged in happiness at work, and what is meant by good work (OECD 2013; Graham & Oswald 2010; Coats & Lekhi 2008; Johnson, Robertson & Cooper 2018). These interests offer researchers the opportunity to review the work on discrete emotions, particularly happiness (Artz, Goodall & Oswald 2016; Warr & Clapperton 2010), and consider the value and explanatory potential it may add to the field of workplace stress.

When, Porter (2008) was asked to 'ponder the future of organizational psychology' (p. 524), he concludes, from his review, that there is 'one thing [he is] certain'; 'going forward, two Cs – context and change – will and should, receive much more concentrated research and scholarly attention than they have up to now. It will be a C×C world!' (p. 525). It is this idea of 'change and context', two not mutually exclusive concepts, where one (change) shapes the other (context), are what, we are trying to express in this first chapter. Change and context are two powerful concepts that have, and are, shaping our discipline, and yet the explanatory power that resides in the context has yet to be exploited fully by researchers. In this instant, perhaps the most significant change – is in our understanding of the changing nature of work. Our understanding of future work arrangements 'is central to filling in a portrait of the new future' (Ashford, George & Blatt 2007, p. 106; Bevan, Brinkley, Bajorek & Cooper 2018).

These new forms of work arrangements and their growing significance and prevalence in the labour market (Spreitzer, Cameron & Garrett 2017; Cappelli & Keller 2013) presents 'fundamental challenges for our theory and research about work and workers as well' (Ashford et al., 2007, p. 66). The use of the 'nonstandard' term to describe this change is simply to give a norm 'against which these workers contrast' (Ashford et al., 2007, p. 68). Yet as our knowledge grows about this 'nonstandard' working, we may now wish to abandon the term 'nonstandard', as this type of working, however described, 'is here to stay' and 'firmly rooted in the world of work' (Spreitzer et al., 2017, p. 475). Enter the Gig economy (Mulcahy 2017). The growth of these employment arrangements is now embedded in, and transiting the workforce, and shaping the way work is changing. Leaving workplace commentators and researchers to consider whether their work is actually capturing the realities of the workforce and working life. All 'powerful reasons why companies and managers [and researchers] need to think differently about people and work [as] tectonic shifts are taking place' (Maitland & Thomson 2011, p. 3).

The themes running through the book

These themes have taken root over time, and are essentially a work in progress, building on our work in Dewe and Cooper (2012 & 2017). They represent a platform that allows us to assess and evaluate whether current research is capturing the realities of working lives. These themes also offer a balance to our work; between our 'technical competence' (Lefkowitz 2011, p. 114) and our moral responsibilities to those whose working lives we investigate. These themes 'stem from the world we live in' (Dewe & Cooper 2017, p. 3), challenging not just our technical competence but also our values, professional expectations and the goals we set. They also act both 'implicitly and explicitly to consider the tools [and aspirations we have] and need, when considering the turbulence these forces of change produce' (Dewe & Cooper 2017, p. 3). These themes cannot escape the shadow of the role of an applied discipline and the academic-practitioner debate, but the intention here, is to discuss them, as a means to not just prompt debate but more to offer them as a platform that provides ways to balance the complex sets of responsibilities we have, with the realities we face. These themes include context, relevance, refinement, and the role of meaning in our research.

Context

We begin by exploring the power and explanatory potential of context and its importance to our discipline particularly because of 'the rapidly diversifying nature of work and work settings [as it] can substantially alter the underlying causal dynamics of worker-organizational relations' (Rousseau & Fried 2001, p. 1) and 'because we have entered a widely heralded "new age" where work organizations are undergoing profound changes' (Gephart 2002, p. 327). In fact, this book is almost all about the dynamics of the changing context within which our research is embedded, and the need to 'pay special attention' to understanding the fundamental change that is rapidly consuming our 'research settings' because context is simply 'designed into [our] research' (Rousseau & Fried 2001, pp. 2; 3). We have identified a number of contexts that offer explanatory power and scope when understanding our research results and indeed reminding us that a construct's meaning 'changes over time' (Rousseau & Fried 2001, p. 5), making one of our themes – 'refinement' – a necessary and significant tool that acknowledges the changing context and its role in making our practices and measures relevant.

We have identified four different contexts, although they simply represent just some of the apparent 'variet[ies] of contexts OB researchers encounter' (Rousseau & Fried 2001, p. 2), making context sufficiently important and giving it a sense of relevancy and interpretable understanding to our work. Our four levels of context simply reflect its infinite variety – the first draws attention to the implications as our (a) *work becomes global* and how constructs and concepts are internationalized; the second which intimately impacts on our work is the (b) *changing realities of work* and its future and, the third is the (c) *appraisal process* and the contextual meanings it provides and its explanatory potential while, the fourth is (d) *methods* – they too set a context and set boundaries through, at times, the traditions they impose (Dewe & Cooper 2017, p. 199). Research settings (context) are significantly important to all phases of the research process, helping to provide meaning to the findings (Rousseau & Fried 2001).

An expanded view of relevance

None of these themes are mutually exclusive, and each is best viewed as an essential part, which reflects a potential platform that brings together those tools 'to understand the meaning of organizational behaviour' (Rousseau & Fried 2001, p. 5). The second of our themes is the *concept of relevance*. We begin by exploring its nature and dimensions, which illustrates its significance to our discipline. A process that we have begun before when we discussed relevance as having '*an inner side* [the changing realities of work] and an *outer side* [working] through an "interactive process" of discovery with managers what is of important to them' (Dewe & Cooper 2017, p. 201; Gulati 2007, p. 780). Now we expand and refine our understanding of relevance but using those, 'two sides' of relevance to build a three-dimensional description of its facets. The first involves (a) *technical competence* – 'its scientific and theoretical underpinnings' (Lefkowitz 2011, p. 112). The second dimension involves (b) *problem solving* – this involves what Corley and Gioia describe as 'prescience' – 'a process of discerning what we need to know and influencing the intellectual framing of what we need to know to enlighten both academic and reflective practitioner domains' (2011, p. 23). What Vermeulen describes as adding a 'second loop' 'in generating insight practitioners find useful for understanding their own organizations and situations better before' (2007, p. 755); and what Gulati describes as 'boundary spanning – research focused squarely on phenomena of interest to managers' (2007, p. 775). The final dimension involves (c) our *moral and ethical responsibilities* to those whose working lives we investigate. Relevance is 'a long-standing theme', but there is little evidence that we have 'paid serious attention to' it (Corley & Gioia 2011, p. 21).

But while relevance as a concept has been rather driven into the shadows by its first two dimensions (Lefkowitz 2008), in a dramatically changing context the power and authority of this third dimension cannot be ignored. This third dimension ensures that we are fulfilling our moral and ethical responsibilities to those whose working lives we investigate by understanding the realities of work and acknowledging their experiences. It is this third dimension that offers our work balance, a sensegiving, sensemaking focus and meaning, by maintaining a 'humanist' values perspective which Lefkowitz (2008, p. 441) argues gives our work that 'empathy for much of what workers in fact experience on the job' (Lefkowitz 2011, p. 113). Relevance, particularly its third dimension, must become a crucial part of the research process if we are to develop useful knowledge; meaning knowledge that captures the changing realities of work and their impact on well-being.

Refinement and the changing nature of robustness and meaning

Refinement 'is about ensuring that measures reflect the realities of the work experience' (Dewe & Cooper 2017, p. 200), and is intimately linked with relevance. Both relevance and refinement are qualities and components that give new meaning to robustness and, indeed, give new meaning to 'reliability'; measures can be reliable but are they relevant – that is the question we should now be asking (Dewe & Cooper 2017). As we have mentioned before (Dewe & Cooper 2017), measures are attached to a context and so their relevance and meaning comes from that context. The issue is that in a world of 'perpetual motion' (Baruch & Hind 1999, p. 295) measures can, only for a time, describe a construct rather than define it (*see* Dewe & Cooper 2017, p. 139). This means that our themes signal the dimensions that offer our research meaning. The themes are all intimately linked and, as a collective, give our work a sense of balance and relevance. It may be, that, by building on the work of Lefkowitz (2008; 2011) the dimensions discussed could be divided into *values* (our moral responsibilities) and *technical competence* (its scientific and theoretical underpinnings, and its problem focus), and argue that now is the time to be 'conscious' of our values remembering our responsibilities to those who working live we study. Values and technical competence are not mutually exclusive but both are necessary to ensure that our work has meaning, relevancy and balance.

The plan of the book

Chapter 2

We begin Chapter 2 by acknowledging the way technology has shaped our discipline by introducing the idea of 'cyber behaviours', offering a new focus to our discipline – 'cyberpsychology' (Dewe & Cooper 2017, p. 5). From the ever-growing literature of cyberpsychology researchers have explored behaviours and constructs like technostress, problematic internet use (Chiang & Su 2012), dependency and addiction (Griffiths 1995; 2010), cyberslacking and cyberloafing (Lim & Chen 2012), and cyberbullying (Baruch 2005) to mention a few. Our aim in this chapter is to argue that it is through the lens of behaviour that gives a more potent understanding of technology's impact, and the 'emerging realities of contemporary work' (Dewe & Cooper 2017, p. 5). Adopting a 'behavioural approach' to understanding technology's impact we build on and develop a number of themes that emerge from the literature; expanding our understanding of the depth and scope of the behavioural impact of technology. Four themes emerge: (a) *the power, reach and significance of technology* – 'what is clear that the scale of transformation is as great as any witnessed in the past' (Gratton 2014, p. 19); (b) *its significance for behaviour* – 'we make our technologies, and they, in turn, change us' (Turkle 2012, p. 19); (c) *its impact on behaviour* – 'is technology reducing our humanity' (Watson 2018, p. 3); 'is technology offer[ing] us substitutes for connecting with each other face to face' (Turkle 2012, p. 11); 'humans were always far better at inventing tools than using them wisely' (Harari 2018, p. 7); (d) *the choices we face* – 'so of every technology we must ask, does it serve our human purpose?' (Turkle 2012, p. 19); 'the shape of tomorrow is fashioned today' (Donkin 2010, p. 11) and 'it's just progress, I guess. But progress towards what?' (Watson 2018, p. 5). And perhaps there is (e) *a counter-culture emerging* (Digital Minimalism) (Newport 2019) and Deep Work – 'Professional activities performed in a state of [digital] distraction-free concentration' (Newport 2016, p. 3), Free tech Days (Watson 2018, p. 181), and 'more mindful usage of technology' (Colbert, Yee & George 2016, p. 736).

We explore these themes by first setting a context through the idea of 'fourth dimension humans' – 'we have a [digital] *everywhereness* to us now that inevitably alters our relationship[s]' (Scott 2016, p. 4). 'This [digital] intermittent everywhereness has come to seem an ordinary aspect of human behaviour' (Scott 2016, p. 17). In our fourth dimensional world, do we 'expect **more** from technology and **less** from each other' (Turkle 2012 – sub title of book). What sort of world do we want 'from technology and what are we willing to do to accommodate it?' (Turkle 2012, p. 13). In this fourth dimensional world, is the boundary between virtual and reality merging; changing relationships, connectivity and time and place? These behaviours, and the technology that is motivating them give us a broader canvas to explore and yet, a more intimate expression of technology's impact and now needs to be incorporated into our research as they represent the world that work is embedded in. This is what Shadbolt and Hampson call 'our hyper-complex habitat'; and 'a crucial component' of this habitat 'is the multiple layers of networks that sustain us' (2018, p. 26).

There are, of course, other powerful emerging technologies that will transform not just our behaviour but our working lives, communities and societies. For example, robotics and artificial intelligence, machine learning, augmented reality, analytics and algorithms, drones, the internet of things, and wearable and smart clothing. This chapter explores these in terms of a number of themes: (a) *advances in technology stand poised* – to 'transform the everyday nature of our work and the way we communicate' and 'that technological capacity is … a key determinant of the ground rules within which the games of human civilisation gets played out' (Gratton 2014, p. 27); 'Yet there are good reasons to think that this time it is different, and that machine learning will be a real game changer' (Harari 2018, p. 19); (b) *technology will continue to improve and continue to transform the meaning of work* – (Harari 2018); (c) *while we may speculate about technologies impact* – 'however we cannot allow ourselves to be complacent' (Harari 2018, p. 33).

The management literature, where managers are managing technological innovations also illustrates, through a number of themes, the emergence of what may become, the foundations for best practice. These themes include: (a) *an incremental approach is advised* – success is achieved by adopting 'a "low hanging fruit" [approach] that enhance business processes' (Davenport & Ronanki 2019, p. 2); (b) *developing trust in the technology* – 'the message for managers is that helping humans to trust thinking machines will be essential' (Frick 2019, p. 147); (c) *Collaboration is advised* – 'a good person plus a good algorithm is far superior to the best person or the best algorithm alone' ... 'We need them to work together' (Lake 2019, p. 28); 'we believe that combining the capabilities of machines with humans' distinctive strengths will lead to far greater productivity and more value creation' (Porter & Heppelmann 2019, p. 76); (d) *understanding technologies risks and limitation* – 'the challenge for us is to understand their risks and limitations and, through effective management, unlock their remarkable potential' (Luca, Kleinberg & Mullainathan 2019, p. 38); 'We are all wrong sometimes – even the algorithm. The important thing is that we keep learning from that' (Lake 2019, p. 28).

These sentiments allow the chapter to end by offering the issues that researchers need to consider and confront if we are to understand the context of working lives and the moral and ethical responsibilities we have, to those whose working lives we research. We are not describing people as 'hardwired' and 'networked', but researchers are already describing people like machines with robotic qualities – so this must inevitably lead to one of the issues we face as deciding and giving more attention to 'what it is we, as individuals and institutions want to happen' (Watson 2018, p. xv).

Chapter 3

Chapter 3 begins by exploring the multitude ways contemporary society has been described. Perhaps reinforcing the view that we live in an 'age of bewilderment' (Harari 2018, p. xiii). Not forgetting the other ways it has been described, including, 'knowledge economies' now more succinctly described as a 'weightless economy' – a 'term that has stood the test of time' (Coyle & Quah 2002, p. 8). Then there are those that capture the significance of the exponential speed and growth of technological innovation describing our age as 'the second machine age' (Brynjolfsson & McAfee 2014), to 'the fourth industrial revolution' (Schwab 2018b). Even more descriptors capture the technological age that we live in. These include 'connectivity' and the 'Gig economy' (Mulcahy 2017), 'the age of context' (Scoble & Israel 2014) and the need to define generations as 'digital natives, and digital immigrants', (Colbert, Yee & George 2016, p. 731) and the 'internet generation' (Donkin 2010, p. 6). Moreover, perhaps, influenced by the positive psychology movement, 'economies of kindness' (Ardern 2019). All grappling with, in one way or another, the changing nature of work – 'future work' – and the 'approaches and skills required to make the transition to more effective ways of managing people and organizing work for the overall benefit of business, individuals and society' (Maitland & Thomson 2011, p. 3).

'Change' as Ashford, George & Blatt (2007, p. 67) suggest 'is clearly afoot'. 'We have entered a widely heralded "new age" where work organizations are undergoing profound changes' (Gephart 2002, p. 327) leading researchers needing to investigate 'what is actually going on in the sphere of life under study' (Blumer 1969, p. 39). This points us not only to evaluate our traditional views of work, but also 'what models, theories or conceptions of meaning can help us understand changes in the meaning of the workplace and work?' (Gephart 2002, p. 328). This chapter explores the changing nature of work and discusses, in the face of these changes, what this means for how we capture the 'new' realities of work and what that means for concepts like employability (Fugate & Kinicki 2008), the skills needed for the 21st century and working lives (Kivunja 2015), life-long learning, and the sustaining of working lives (Spreitzer, Porath & Gibson 2012). If, 'employees in full-time jobs aren't the future of work' (Mulcahy 2017, p. 187) and, as there has been, 'extraordinary growth in contingent employment arrangements' (Marler, Barringer & Milkovich 2002, p. 425), terms like 'nonstandard', have been used as a means to simply give a norm 'against which these workers contrast' (Ashford *et al.*, 2007, p. 68). As our understanding grows around the changing nature of work, so does the way we discuss it, using terms like 'contingent workers', 'alternative working arrangements' (Spreitzer *et al.*, 2017, p. 475), 'boundaryless and traditional contingent employees' (Marler *et al.*, 2002, p. 425) and, of course the Gig economy (Mulcahy 2017). All these authors acknowledge this type of 'nonstandard' work, however described, 'is here to stay' and 'firmly rooted in the world of work' (Spreitzer *et al.*, 2017, p. 475). 'In the future the "new" work and workplace will no longer be new' (Gephart 2002, p. 328) so we explore what employment arrangements best express the realities of working in the new millennium.

In general, two themes emerge that capture the nature of this millennium working style. These themes are 'flexibility, feasibility, the nature of the work performed, technology and changing worker preferences' (Ashford *et al.*, 2007, pp. 76–79). Others point to the importance of 'flexibility'; 'flexibility in the employment relationship, flexibility in the scheduling of work and flexibility in where work is accomplished' (Spreitzer *et al.*, 2017, p. 473). As Mulcahy points out 'where once were *jobs*, there is increasingly just *work*' (2017, p. 6). The consequences of these changes to work means that 'people will have more jobs during their careers, and more careers during their working lives', and 'individuals will rely more heavily on marketing their unique skills, reputation and "personal brand"' (Maitland & Thomson 2011, pp. 152; 153). This means that these changes 'have enormous implications about how we think about managing our careers and structuring our lives' (Mulcahy 2017, p. 3). Not forgetting the implications for theory, our models and measures, and our discipline as the context and reality of working lives is significantly changed.

Nevertheless, the working context is changing in other ways, and if organizations and working lives are in 'perpetual motion' (Baruch & Hind 1999, p. 295) this chapter touches on other textual changes. Including the refinement of capitalism suggested by emphasizing 'compassionate capitalism' with its focus on individual flourishing (Myers 2007), and 'responsible capitalism' that has the aim of bringing organizations and communities closer together through developing a 'strong[er] sense of place' and a 'more collaborate ethos' (Stears & Parker 2012, pp. 3–8). Not forgetting the globalization of the concept of well-being and the ideas that GNP now needs to be re-defined. To include issues like well-being (even Gross National Wellbeing), and those aspects that reflect values and issues that shape the quality of life giving a greater sense as a measure of social progress and those 'aspects of life that matter to people' (OECD 2013, p. 2; Stiglitz, Sen & Fitoussi 2009). The chapter ends by exploring what these changes mean for work stress research. Pointing to the crucial role that context plays in our understanding of the stress process. Illustrating the importance of refining measures, particularly stressors by examining their relevance to the realities of working life and the direction that research needs to take to ensure our ethical responsibilities are meet to those whose working lives we investigate.

Chapter 4

Chapter 4 begins by emphasizing how fundamental our understanding of how people cope is to work stress research (Dewe & Cooper 2017) with researchers already, showing a 'boundless enthusiasm for' this type of research (Aldwin 2000, p. 73). This is not to suggest that empirical research on coping has been free of controversy, particularly when questions of measuring strategies are the focus of debate (Coyne & Racioppo 2000). Perhaps, coping research derives its importance to us, as researchers, simply because there is this sense of 'immediate personal relevance' (Aldwin 2000, p. 73) that comes with it. Coping research has emphasized the importance of being 'sensitive to the complexities [when] measuring' strategies by developing our understanding through the frameworks we derive to classify them (Dewe & Cooper 2017, p. 143).

Four reasons make classifying strategies empirically strategic. The first is that 'classifying strategies' is described as an evolving process as classification frameworks represents, at any one time, our state of knowledge (Folkman 2011). The second reason, qualitatively different to the first, illustrates the fundamental role that the context plays when classifying coping strategies, so any framework must reflect the realities of contemporary work and work behaviours. The third reason points to the growing interest in well-being through the emphasis on human capital and resource-based strategies – 'competing through people' (Dewe & Cooper 2017, p. 15). The fourth reason flows from the growing 'digital fluency' of the workforce, and our developing understanding of cyberbehaviours (Colbert et al., 2016, p. 733).

In this chapter, our focus is to explore the role that cyberbehaviours like cyberloafing (Lim 2002; Lim & Chen 2012), may play in expanding our view of coping strategies and fulfil a need to explore and perhaps adopt in our classification framework, a coping strategy that reflects cyberbehaviours. Researchers have already begun to explore the idea of 'redesigning work for a digital workforce', and 'leveraging' the 'mindful usage of technology in ways that promote time for focused thinking, opportunities for recovery, and effective collaborations' (Colbert et al., 2016, p. 735). All perhaps expressing technologies role as a coping strategy. We also, in this chapter, as we have before (Dewe & Cooper 2012; 2017), emphasize the fundamental importance of the process of primary appraisal – the meanings given to stressful encounters – in coping research and work stress generally. 'Appraisals' are the context within which coping strategies are embedded. Their explanatory power is reflected in Snyder's comments 'I believe that it is incumbent upon each proponent of a new coping theory to explicate the nature of the appraisal process' (1999, p. 331).

The chapter also turns to the positive psychology movement (Seligman & Csikszentmihalyi 2000), and its influence on coping research. Pointing to the need to investigate the role of positive outcomes and emotions; following on from the dictum from Lazarus & Cohen-Charash that 'discrete emotions are the "coin of the realm" in coping research' (2001, p. 45). Here we are drawn to explore the interest in the concept of happiness, and its potential relationship with coping. The chapter also explores the question somewhat ignored but frequently inferentially acknowledged, of what we mean by coping effectiveness (Dewe & Cooper 2017). The chapter concludes by taking up the issues of refinement and relevance that gives coping research its power, significance, meaning and credibility allowing us to better understand the potential of coping research. Reinforcing how the 'stress and the coping narrative evolves with the accumulation of research findings' (Folkman 2011, p. 461).

Chapter 5

Chapter 5 returns us to the themes running through this book. All the themes collectively give a framework for evaluating our progress. The themes also give collectively, a sense of balance to our work. Each knit together to form a platform that is sensitive to our responsibilities to those whose working lives we study. There is a danger of course in singling out just one theme. But since we have adopted a broad canvas when considering the meaning of relevance, because of its potential potency and significance, particularly at a time: (1) when organizations are in a state of 'perpetual motion' (Baruch & Hind 1999, p. 295), (2) working lives are being dramatically reshaped, (3) the way technology is having a profound impact on peoples' behaviour; meaning that communicating and building relations has been significantly refined. All giving new meaning and importance to the significance of relevance. Moreover, it now needs to be given a more central role in framing our research to ensure that our work meets our responsibilities to those whose working lives we study. This helps to emphasize the nature of what it means to be an applied discipline, and gives voice to the 'empathy to what workers in fact experience on the job' (Lefkowitz 2011, p. 113). This is why relevance is intimately linked to context, refinement and the meanings of our research. This chapter, and indeed this book, points to the power and authority that 'relevance' and its associated themes, have; hopefully capturing the spirit and the values of our applied discipline. The chapter concludes by expressing, as a powerful reminder, not just where our theories are taking us, but how well they express the realities of working lives and where change should be directed.

Chapter 2

Technology, behaviour and work stress

We begin Chapter 2 by acknowledging the way technology has shaped our discipline by introducing the idea of 'cyberbehaviours' offering a new focus for our discipline – 'cyberpsychology' (Dewe & Cooper 2017, p. 5). From the ever-growing literature of cyberpsychology, researchers have explored, for example, behaviours and constructs like technostress (Ragu-Nathan, Tarafdar & Ragu-Nathan 2008; Tarafdar, Cooper & Stich 2019), and problematic internet use (Chiang & Su 2012), dependency and addition (Griffiths 1995; 2010), cyberslacking and cyberloafing (Lim & Chen 2012), and cyberbullying (Baruch 2005). Our aim in this chapter is to argue that it is through the lens of behaviour that gives a more potent understanding of technology's impact and the 'emerging realities of contemporary work' (Dewe & Cooper 2017, p. 5). Adopting a 'behavioural approach' to understanding technology's impact, we build on and develop a number of themes that emerge from the literature; expanding our understanding of the depth and scope of the behavioural impact of technology.

Four themes emerge: (a) *the power, reach and significance of technology* – 'what is clear that the scale of transformation is as great as any witnessed in the past' (Gratton 2012, p. 19); others see it 'without parallel in history' (Shadbolt & Hampson 2018, p. 58); (b) *its significance for behaviour* – 'we make our technologies, and they, in turn, change us' (Turkle 2012, p. 19); (c) *its impact on behaviour* – 'is technology reducing our humanity' (Watson 2018, p. 3); 'is technology offer[ing] us substitutes for connecting with each other face to face' (Turkle 2012, p. 11); 'humans were always far better at inventing tools than using them wisely' (Harari 2018, p. 7); (d) *the choices we face* – 'so of every technology we must ask, does it serve our human purposes?' (Turkle 2012, p. 19); 'the shape of tomorrow is fashioned today' (Donkin 2010, p. 10); and 'it's progress, I guess. But progress towards what?' (Watson 2018, p. 5). And perhaps there is (e) *a counter-culture emerging* (Digital Minimalism (Newport 2019) and Deep Work – 'Professional activities performed in a state of [digital] distraction-free concentration' (Newport 2016, p. 3), Free Tech Days (Watson 2018, p. 181), and 'more mindful usage of technology' (Colbert, Yee & George 2016, p. 736).

Setting a context: in a digital saturated age

We explore these themes by first setting a context through the idea of 'fourth dimension humans' – 'we have a [digital] *everywhereness* to us now that inevitably alters our relationship[s]' (Scott 2016, p. 4). 'This [digital] intermittent everywhereness has come to seem an ordinary aspect of human behaviour' (Scott 2016, p. 17). In our fourth dimensional world do we 'expect **more** from the technology and **less** from each other' (Turkle 2012 – sub title of book). What sort of world do we want 'from technology and what are we willing to do to accommodate it?' (Turkle 2012, p. 13). In this fourth-dimension world, will this 'demand an evolution in how we think about what it means to be present' (Scott 2016, p. 14) with the 'meaning of presence [shifting] from physically being there to the psychological experience of being there' (Colbert *et al.*, 2016, p. 737). '[Are] we now witnessing a remapping of "here" and "there"' (Scott 2016, p. 15)? Does this '[digital] everywhereness' begin to soften the boundaries between virtual and reality, and change how we establish and manage relationships? What do we now mean by connectivity, and what happens to the traditional meanings and understanding we give to concepts like time and place; '[are we] in a world that is both everywhere and nowhere' (Scott 2016, p. 21)?

Does the title of Turkle's book sum up where we are at; 'Alone together' (2018, p. 1)? Are we 'already dissolving the supposedly hard distinction between what's real and what's not real, and in so doing changing ourselves and, possibly, human nature' (Watson 2018, p. 22)? This is what Shadbolt and Hampson (2018, p. 26) call 'our hyper-complex habitat'; and a 'crucial component' of this habitat 'is the layers of networks that sustains us'. 'Technology reshapes the landscape of our emotional lives, but is it offering us the lives we want to lead?' (Turkle 2012, p. 17). Paraphrasing the words of Turkle it is not 'what [technology does] for us but what [it does] to us, to our ways of thinking about ourselves, our relationships, our sense of being human'

(2012, p. 2). 'All of us make daily use of devices that are a *million* times more powerful than any machine of the 1970s' (Shadbolt & Hampson 2018, pp. 24–25).

When you think about the extraordinary growth and range of technologies and networks which are constantly tumbling over themselves to get our attention and become instantly available to us, and the scope and impact of social apps and their instant availability (and the demands they make to shape our worlds or even give us another world), the question for us is who is making the demands? Is it the technology or is it us, and how we use them and engage with them? Is it our behaviour that places and drives the demands on us? And since the technologies are always there and always ready, it is completely understandable that our 'current relationship with technology [is] unsustainable' (Newport 2019, p. x). 'We send letters now as email' at an 'overwhelming' volume. The iPhone 'smallness means it can be a constant companion' (Shadbolt & Hampson 2018, pp. 47; 53) – 'the technology has become like a phantom limb, it is so much a part of [us]' (Turkle 2012, p. 17). 'Very quickly, the text message became the connection of choice … – the world of connectivity – to be uniquely suited to the overworked and overscheduled life it makes possible' (Turkle 2012, p. 13). Is this a time that spells 'the end of a certain public etiquette; on the street we speak into the invisible microphones on our mobile phones and appear to be talking to ourselves' (Turkle 2012, p. 16).

No wonder, with even these few examples, you can sense the emerging issues like 'digital distraction' (Watson 2018, p. 15), 'a common term about modern digital life was *exhaustion*', (Newport 2019, p. x), 'declining real-life interactions' (Watson 2018, p. 12), the 'digital hyperconnected decade' (Levitin 2019) and 'the way new technologies seemed to be draining, meaning and satisfaction from [people's] time spent outside of work' (Newport 2019, p. x). In this 'networked age' and 'the clamour for online attention', if we place more and more of ourselves and our lives on social media and other networks then it raises the question of 'who owns the future' – are we, as Lanier suggests, 'the uncompensated sources of the data that make networks valuable in the first place' (Lanier 2014, pp. xvi; xix; xxi)? Then there is what has been described as 'life mix' – 'the life mix is the mash-up of what you have on- and offline'. 'So now we have the idea of multilifing.' Now, 'one moves into the virtual with fluidity and on the go' (Turkle 2012, p. 160).

The emerging counter-culture

Two questions, at least, emerge from this digital saturated age; the first, does this herald the beginnings of a counter-culture, and the second, what does this mean for work stress research? A counter-culture is on the horizon and quickly developing. Perhaps the seeds were sown when organizations were encouraged to consider the issue of the 'mindful usage of technology', and while strategies like 'technology-free meetings' 'may have the benefit of increasing empathy as compared to technologically mediated communication methods' (Colbert, Yee & George 2016, pp. 735; 736), more research is needed 'to determine how to most effectively create norms around these [mindful] practices'. Whilst future research is also needed 'to expand our understanding of how social controls work in concert with technological features and organizational polices to' promote the mindful use of technology (Colbert *et al.*, 2016, p. 736).

Other mindful strategies include 'smartphone-free' nights to encourage 'employees to connect with their families and truly recover from the stresses of the day' (Colbert *et al.*, 2016, p. 736), while some organizations are 'on a mission to abolish internal email altogether. They prefer people to walk around and talk to each other' (Watson 2018, p. 181). All these mindful strategies are accompanied by research, and are built around developing workplace initiatives. Interestingly some workplaces are offering 'no track' initiatives where, in those organizations' employees' movements are tracked (Watson 2018, p. 181). On the other hand, life insurers are offering rewards and programmes 'that encourages' those insured 'to live healthier lifestyles' some using a tracking device – a fitbit – 'to encourage healthier lives', and ensure that they are sticking to their healthy regime (Flaws & Pullar-Strecker 2019, p. 22). Reflecting somewhat, the yin and yang of technology.

Digital minimalism

Other 'counter-culture' strategies, with perhaps a touch of mindfulness in mind reflect the problem of 'digital distraction' (Newport 2016; 2019; Watson 2018, p. 15). While 'willpower, tips and vague resolutions are not sufficient by themselves to tame the ability of new technologies to invade [our] cognitive landscape' (Newport 2019, p. xiv), this sentiment, convinced Newport, 'that what you need instead is a full-fledged *philosophy of technology use*' (2019, p. xiv). This leads to two thoroughly researched and evaluated programmes described as – '*digital minimalism*' (Newport 2019) and '*deep work*' (Newport 2016). With digital minimalism the first step when adopting the philosophy ('it applies the belief that *less can be more* to our relationship with digital tools' (2019, p. xv) the first principle is the '*digital declutter*' – this has three aspects (a) *clutter is costly* (particularly in terms of time wasted), (b) *optimization is important* (select only those that supports what you value then considering '*how* you use it'), (c) *intentionality is satisfying* (acting more and being intentional rather than giving way to convenience 'in the way [you] engage with new technologies') (2019, pp. 35–36). In these three initial steps, the message is, you can now identify and define those technologies that are optional and clutter your lifestyle and so the system is ready for you to begin to engage in the 'declutter process' (2019, p. 60). Newport, goes on to outline the steps that need to be taken to initiate the 'digital declutter process' and to 'adopt this lifestyle' (2019, pp. 60; 59).

Solitude in a digital saturated age

Newport (2019, pp. 93–94) also points to the 'value of solitude', a commodity, that in this digital saturated age, 'is starting to fade away altogether' and 'that people might forget this state of being altogether' (2019, pp. 99; 101). In many ways, solitude gives us the opportunity 'to be free from input from other minds', where you are with your own thoughts; providing a context to clarifying them and focusing 'on your own thoughts and experiences' (2019, pp. 93–94). We have, Newport writes, reached in this 'hyperconnected age' Levitin (2019) a state of almost 'solitude deprivation' (2019, p. 99). Newport's focus on the therapeutic properties of solitude resonates with work stress research, as it has the hallmarks of an autogenic (self-generating) technique similar to the relaxation response and meditation. In the future, researchers may wish to investigate the idea of solitude and its explanatory potential in its role as a coping strategy. Remember that autogenic techniques also require lifestyle changes, and when this age describes people as hardwired, 'simply put, humans are not wired to be constantly wired', and those who understand 'the key to thriving in our high-tech world, they've learned, is to spend less time using technology' (Newport 2019, pp. 109; xv).

The point is, in a digital saturated age, it is inevitable for many to focus on the choice's technology offers, rather than the life it is crafting for them. This is why autogenic techniques are important, even if their potency has been ignored or, even more likely, discarded in the hurly-burly of our digital lives. Why are they important? Because they consciously require lifestyle changes and then require deliberately putting time aside away from busy schedules to engage in them. So, as our knowledge of our digital lives continues to develop, it is surely time for stress researchers to rejuvenate their interest in these types of coping techniques, whose benefit rest in putting back reflection, into what are digitally busy lives, providing time to think and generally freeing your mind 'to focus on your own thoughts and experiences' (Newport 2019, p. 94), perhaps avoiding the anguish of 'The love affair is over. It's the end of a rose-filtered era. I have decided I'm breaking up with social media. And honestly, it feels like it's been coming for a while ...' (Johnson 2019, p. 16).

Deep work

Newport also introduces us to what he describes as 'deep work' – 'Professional activities performed in a state of distraction-free concentration that push your cognitive capabilities to their limit' (2016, p. 3). What this means is that the learned skill of intense concentration on a cognitively demanding task requires a totally 'focused intensity without distraction'. 'To learn, in other words, is an act of deep work' (Newport 2016, p. 37). Newport signals what is a fundamental skill for the 21st century – the *ability to learn to learn*. So, in an age of digital saturation, 'deep work is [often] exiled in favour of more distracting high-tech behaviours' (2016, p. 69) forgoing the productivity and learning benefits that this type of work produces. As Newport (2016, pp. 81; 85) points out, contemporary work has plenty of 'shallow concerns' like 'emails ... that vie for [our] attention' and which limit our focus and concentration and perhaps, even, prescribe our ability to learn. Future research may wish to build these ideas about deep work when investigating and thinking about topics like job design.

Newport also turns to the tyranny of 'busyness as a proxy for productivity' – 'doing lots of stuff in a visible manner'; 'a mindset' that works to destroys creating deep work behaviours, again ignoring the productivity and learning benefits that makes deep work more mindful and satisfying (Newport 2016, p. 64). Interestingly, technology itself may give us a lesson when thinking about deep work by considering 'versions of machine learning ([with their capacity for] deep learning, in particular ...)', may set the mark for individuals to urgently recapture that mindset that rekindles those skills for practicing deep learning

(Davenport & Ronanki 2019, p. 6). Newport points to Csikszentmihalyi's (1990) work on flow to express the nature of deep work. In describing Csikszentmihalyi's 1990 work on flow, Burke (2002) describes it as 'a state in which individual's become so involved in an activity that nothing else matters' (p. 91). It seems, in this sentence he is envisioning a construct that expresses the nature and, perhaps, the power of deep work. Newport (2016) concludes his work by setting out the rules for individuals to achieve this deep work state.

Mindful use of technology

Finally, in terms of a counter culture, there are organizations considering 'how to encourage mindful usage of technology'. There are, it seems, a number of options. The first 'is to determine how to most effectively create norms' around the practices that represent mindful behaviours (Colbert et al., 2016, p. 736). For example, how extensive do the norms have to be which leads to how do you manage, supervise and govern and 'remind people of appropriate usage practices' particularly if those practices occur away from work. While, Colbert and her colleagues, suggest that 'while it is possible that individuals can be conditioned to use technology more consciously' there may well need to be 'changes [that have] to come, in the design of the technology itself' to aid altering usage patterns. Another option is to better understand how the social context in conjunction with the technology may aid as a mechanism to shape patterns of behaviour. Finally, it may be that workers themselves 'develop new ways of working that leverage the full capabilities of technology' (Colbert et al., 2016, p. 736). 'Research is needed not only to examine the effects of the growing use of technology by a digital workforce, but also to provide guidance about how best to utilize technology in the service of organizational goals' (Colbert et al., 2016, p. 737).

Other technologies and their context

There are, of course, other powerful emerging technologies that will transform not just our behaviour, but our working lives, communities and societies. For example, robotics and artificial intelligence, machine learning, augmented reality, analytics and algorithms, drones, driverless autonomous cars, the internet of things, and wearable and smart clothing. We begin our discussion of these technologies first through a number of themes: (a) *how advances in technology stand poised* – 'to transform the everyday nature of our work and the way we communicate' and that technological capacity is ... 'a key determinant of the ground rules within which the games of human civilisation gets played out' (Gratton 2014, p. 27); 'yet there are good reasons to think that this time it is different, and that machine learning will be a real game changer' (Harari 2018, p. 19); (b) *technology will continue to improve and continue to transform the meaning of work* – (Harari 2018); (c) *while we can speculate about technologies impact* – 'however we cannot allow ourselves to be complacent' (Harari 2018, p. 33).

This is the context against which the impact of these technologies will be measured, judged, understood, utilized and developed. While we have choices as to the future we want, 'this technological tidal wave is unprecedented in modern history and it's hard to figure out how humans can respond' raising the question of 'what we might do to make work more people-centric in an age of machines?' (Watson 2018, pp. 173; 181). These are not idle questions, as they are asked to prompt us to think 'about who we are and where we are going and about the need for human beings to remain central to any new digital interests or perspectives' (Watson 2018, p. xv). Whatever happens 'we will be required to make some fundamental shifts in how we think and act our way into our future working lives' (Gratton 2014, p. 19). In:

> this machine age, we need to think more deeply about what it is we really want and what we value, both as individuals and as a society. Our generation has inherited more opportunities to transform the world than any other. That's a cause for optimism, but only if we we're mindful of our choices.
>
> (Brynjolfsson & McAfee 2014, p. 257)

We need, now, 'to engage in strategic dialogues around emerging technologies ... to actively shape the world in line with common human values' (Schwab 2018b, p. x).

The requirement for new leadership styles

In the time of 'emerging technologies – action and leadership are required from all organizations, sectors and individuals in the form of "systems leadership," involving new approaches to technology, governance and values' (Schwab 2018b, p. 220). Systems leadership goes beyond just the design of technology to embrace 'how they are governed and the values they exhibit in how they affect people from all backgrounds' (Schwab 2018a, p. 3). It enables us 'to think more deeply about the relationship between technology and society, understanding the ways in which our collective actions (and inactions) create the future' (Schwab 2018b, p. 220). System leadership 'is about cultivating a shared vision for change – working together with all stakeholders of global society – and then acting on it to change how the system delivers its benefits, and to whom' (Schwab 2018b, p. 221). Values, and the common good, are at the core of 'systems leadership' and it is these, and in working together, that such leadership can create 'a renaissance that is human-centred'. (Schwab 2018b, p. 228). It requires 'considering how our values and perspectives as individuals are shaped and affected by technologies as we make important technology-related decisions' (Schwab 2018b, p. 229). It is about working together as it requires a contribution from all and, from all of us, 'a shift in mindsets' (Schwab 2018b, p. 220).

Indeed, this call for action seems to capture a common theme in the writings of many of the authors cited. As it is, they argue, it is the time for all, to be part of a broader discussion, as these technologies emerge, in how 'to shape [them] in ways that promote the common good, enhance human dignity and protect the environment' (Schwab 2018b, p. x). It is, as Watson explains, 'the relationship and balance of power between humans and machines is a fundamental one for both current and future generations to figure out'. So, he asks, 'why is there such a silence?' He answers his question by pointing to 'perhaps it's because most of us are tethered to mobile devices that constantly distract us and prevent us from thinking deeply about the impact of these technologies' (2018, p. 7). This call for action is a call that we, as researchers need to heed and cannot ignore. It resonates with our focus on relevance, and our responsibilities to those whose working lives we research. It also complements our focus on individual well-being and, for our discipline it surely must relate to its 'human-centred approach [that] empowers individuals' to consider and attend to the impact of technology on us and society (Schwab 2018b, p. 228). It also offers us a focus, and an opportunity, 'by influencing and guiding the systems that surround us and shapes our lives' (Schwab 2018b, p. 8). It requires us to take our research onto a broader canvas that allows us to be part of these 'strategic discussions' and to explore the ways our research can contribute and help direct and shape this debate not forgetting the realities of the world we live in.

Emerging technologies

It is best to begin this section cautiously in line with the arguments advanced above. That is, it is built around the idea that we all have choices about how we shape our world.

> What is happening in technology, innovation and the future of work is not an inexorable process beyond anyone's control. Instead it is the result of choices by politicians, business people and consumers. These choices shape the innovation environment and have profound impacts on what kind of innovation occurs and what impact it has on the world of work.

What is important, is the way we build the synergetic relationship between people and the technology and 'on the kind of society we are aiming for' (Salmon 2019, pp. 14; 15). In this context we explore these emerging technologies.

Cognitive technology: AI – artificial intelligence and machine learning

We begin this journey into emerging technology by issuing another caution, particularly since we begin this journey by exploring the impact of 'cognitive technology: AI artificial intelligence (AI)' and machine learning. Even though, as Davenport and Ronanki (2019) report, that their survey of 'business executives, three quarters of them believed that AI will substantially transform their companies within three years'. Although these authors suggest that an incremental approach 'that enhance[s] business processes' will generate the best success, they go on to add the caution that 'the hype surrounding artificial intelligence has been especially powerful, and some organizations have been seduced by it' (Davenport & Ronanki 2019, pp. 1–2). From their research Davenport and Ronanki 'broadly speaking' identified three types of AI: 'automating business processes (Robotics and cognitive automation), gaining insights through data analysis (cognitive insights), and engaging with customers and employees (cognitive engagement)'. The organizational strategy, these authors suggest, should be first, to 'understand which technologies perform what types of tasks', then 'create a prioritized portfolio of projects based on business needs,' and then 'develop plans to scale up across the company' (2019, pp. 2; 3). This summary cannot capture the richness of these authors analysis nor the challenges and obstacles they identified that await those organizations wishing to engage with this technology, but the power of their work lies in the fact that it is built around organizational executives actually grappling with this technology whilst, at the same time, attempting to establish what good practice would look like. So, they (Davenport & Ronanki) conclude by suggesting that properly planned and developed, 'cognitive technology could usher in a golden age of productivity, work satisfaction, and prosperity' (2019, p. 17). Although this 'golden age' comes with 'no room for complacency on issues of workforce displacement' ... nor the challenge surrounding 'the ethics of smart machines' (2019, p. 17).

It is expected that there would be a variety of views that surround this type of technology, since researchers and commentators are frequently looking into the future and trying to predict the consequences of this sort of technology and how it can be best managed. We explore some of the views attempting to capture this variety. First, there is a sense that the way forward is through 'collaborative intelligence', where 'humans and AI actively enhance each other's complementary strengths'. It is understanding how people 'augment machines', and how machines 'can enhance what humans do best' (Wilson & Daugherty 2019, pp. 127–128). The 'implementation of AI technology also requires a significant commitment to develop employees with what we call "fusion skills" – '[those] that enable them to work effectively at the human-machine interface' (Wilson & Daugherty 2019, p. 142).

It is this type of partnership that sustains and gives power to collaborative intelligence. In a sense, Harari (2018, pp. 22; 29) could well support such an idea when he points to what he describes as the 'two particularly important non-human abilities that AI possesses are connectivity and updateability'. Later, he suggests, that 'instead of humans competing with AI, they could focus on servicing and leveraging AI' and the market may be more likely 'characterised by human-AI cooperation rather than competition'. On the other hand, there is the issue of trust, and the question of 'how can you persuade your team to trust artificial intelligence? Or to accept a robot as a member [of your team] – or even as a manager?' (Frick 2019, p. 146). As Frick suggests, as 'machines evolve from tools to teammates accepting them will be more than a matter of simply adopting some new technology' (2019, p. 147). Do we need to pause from time to time and consider whether we are 'confusing what's possible with what's needed?' (Watson 2018, p. 200).

Is it as Turkle queries, what do we mean when we ask the question of 'what is a relationship?' When we think about humans and robots, do we also ask 'what are we willing to give up when we turn to robots rather than humans?' (2012, pp. 19–20). The 'key question' Cowen argues, is: 'Are you good at working with intelligent machines or not?' (2014, p. 4). What happens, Turkle muses, 'when machine intelligence crosses a tipping point?' when 'artificial intelligence will go beyond anything we can currently conceive' (2012, p. 25). The same point is made by Harari (2018, p. 30) although in the context of whether any jobs will be safe 'because machine learning and robotics will continue to improve'. As 'our technologies are racing ahead but many of our skills and organizations are lagging behind ... [so, we must] come up with strategies that allow human workers to race ahead with machines instead of racing against them' (Brynjolfsson & McAfee 2011, p. 9). Re-enforcing that 'we cannot allow ourselves to be complacent' (Harari 2018, p. 33). Yet as Salmon argues, as 'we will likely see significant technological change. Now is the time to think about what we need to do to create the future of work we might actually want' (2019, p. 130).

We begin this task by remaining with the management literature, where managers are making choices in organizations working with intelligent machines and AI, and we illustrate through a number of themes that emerge from that literature what may yet become, through these first tentative steps, a framework for good practice. These themes include: (a) *an incremental approach is advised* – success is achieved by adopting 'a "low hanging fruit" [approach] that enhance business processes' (Davenport & Ronanki 2019, p. 2), (b) *developing trust in the technology* – 'the message for managers is that helping humans to trust thinking machines will be essential' (Frick 2019, p. 147); (c) *collaboration is advised* – 'a good person plus a good algorithm is far superior to the best person or the best algorithm alone' ... 'We need them to work together' (Lake 2019, p. 28); 'we believe that combining the capabilities of machines with human strengths will lead to far greater productivity and more value creation' (Porter & Heppelmann 2019, p. 76); (d) *understanding technologies risks and limitation* – 'the challenge for us is to understand their risks and limitations and, through effective management, unlock their remarkable potential' (Luca, Kleinberg & Mullainathan 2019, p. 38); 'We are all wrong sometimes – even the algorithm. The important thing is that we keep learning from that' (Lake 2019, p. 28).

A pause to catch our breath and think about what this means for work stress research

It is time to take our research onto a broader canvas and begin to explore and think about ways we can shape our idea about future work, and how we build the synergetic relationship between people and the technology. Our understanding of this relationship must be expressed and set within a context that is people-centric, focused on well-being, relevant and captures the realities of work. We need, for example, to begin by exploring what we mean by a relationship and how is it collaborative. To get closer to what we mean by a relationship, and how it becomes collaborative, is to think in terms of training and development or more particularly learning and development. What skills are required, taking the idea of 'fusion skills' (Wilson & Daugherty 2019, p. 142), and building on this idea allowing for work on what sort of training and learning is required and how that learning transfers and expresses the relationship we aspire too. It will need commitment where 'tomorrows leaders will instead be those that embrace collaborative intelligence, transforming their operations, their markets, their industries, and – no less important – their workforces' (Wilson & Daugherty 2019, p. 143). We can also take a lead from the work of Wilson and Daugherty when they show how 'smart machines are helping humans expand their abilities' (2019, pp. 131–138). Similarly, as Schwab suggests, 'the biggest impact of AI and robotics on the future of work will be the automation of a range of repetitive or technical tasks, freeing up people's time for more interpersonal and creative work' (2018, p. 132).

It also means that we need to think about the relationship in terms of Cowen's question 'Are you good at working with intelligent machines or not?' (2014, p. 4), distilling those factors that make us 'good or not' and, in this context thinking about the role that trust, acceptance of the technology, and our understanding of the challenges, risks and limitations of those technologies, plays in establishing the relationship. Establishing the facets of such a relationship has implications for some of our traditional measures of stressors, like role ambiguity and role conflict, and so there is a place for these measures to be refined taking into account the issues of technology and the way they express the changing role of workers. The shadow that these smart machines cast over work begs the questions what will happen to jobs? This is what Watson describes, as 'the "will it, won't it" question surrounding automation and unemployment'. Watson adds though, if we are smart enough to create machines that get rid of jobs 'there's no reason to suppose' we can't use those creative talents to 'invent new forms of work' (2018, p. 176). We will take this issue up in the next chapter and discuss these arguments in the context of employability and what skills and learning will be needed for a digital saturated age.

Turning back to other emerging technologies: augmented reality (AR) and algorithms

We begin by turning our attention to augmented reality (AR), as 'this will become the new interface between humans and machines'. AR's power lies in its ability to convert 'data and analytics into images that are overlaid on the real world'. This technology is already in 'dozens of car models' but its power and authority lies in the way it can transform, 'supplement or replace traditional manuals and training methods at an ever-faster pace' (Porter & Heppelmann 2019, p. 54), reduces 'cognitive distance and minimizes cognitive load' because its power lies in being able 'to process the physical and digital simultaneously' … enhancing and speeding 'our ability to absorb and act on' information (Porter & Heppelmann 2019, pp. 57; 55). The combination of 'the capabilities of machines with humans' distinctive strengths' offers opportunities to increase productivity' and more value creation. 'We see AR as a historic innovation that provides this' (Porter & Heppelmann 2019, p. 76). Porter and Heppelmann offer 'a roadmap' for how organizations can position AR and 'the essential questions companies face' (2019, pp. 54; 67) when thinking about AR and strategy. But AR certainly dramatically changes and has altered the way we think about training and development. Researchers should look at whether the transfer of learning is more effective using AR materials since they reduce the 'cognitive distance'. Similarly, research should also consider its potential to improve decision making and value creation.

Managers are 'turning more and more' to algorithms to make business decisions. The message seems to be the same: managers need to understand their limitations, as it is through this understanding that 'effective management' will emerge. Part of this understanding is acknowledging how algorithms behave. They are 'literal, meaning that they'll do exactly what you ask them to do. And they're black boxes, meaning' they are short on explaining why 'they offer particular recommendations'. So, 'algorithms need manager[s] too', to 'be explicit about [their] goals' and 'making sure' they have chosen the 'right data inputs'. The best approach for managers is to be 'crystal clear about everything you want to achieve' (Luca *et al.*, 2019, pp. 29; 31; 32; 35; 38). Ultimately, the art, it seems, lies in the collaboration between the machine and the manager.

Internet of things, wearables and smart clothing

The internet of things 'will drive deeper connectivity in every part of life, link together global economies in novel ways and likely encompass a burgeoning machine-to-machine economy as well' (Schwab 2018b, p. 99). It comes, however, with 'challenges, risks and dangers'. There needs, for example, to be a world-wide initiative to establish protocols and procedures accompanied with values and standards because without these 'the potential of [the internet of things] is threatened'. The risks go beyond just organizational risks, but risks to 'users and the public', where challenges await its management and the development of new business models. 'Cybersecurity is a standout risk', and will need to be managed across international boundaries and risks range from 'data privacy, protecting consumers, sharing data and issues of intimidation, theft, harm or ransom' and the stability of the system and its impact on work, employment and skills (Schwab 2018b, pp. 105–106). 'The real value in [the] internet of things development lies in data collection, analysis and management, finding unexpected correlations and opportunities, and anticipating disruption trends' (Schwab 2018b, p. 109).

The winner when exploring smart clothing may well be health. For example, 'the University of Bristol is developing "smart trousers" with artificial muscles which give frail people bionic strength so they can live independently for longer' (The Dominion Post 2018, p. 20). Another innovation is 'Patients can wear hardware. The wearable device … where every two seconds it captures vital signs … If signs of deterioration are spotted medical staff are alerted' (Kobie 2018, pp. 2/4–3/4). It seems that health will also benefit from robotics and machine learning and that there 'has never been a more exciting time in healthcare innovation [as those two technologies] drive improved outcomes'. The idea of 'new generation digital surgery' is closing fast but in these heady innovative times 'the importance of keeping the patient at the very core of what we do' where 'the importance of touch, empathy and that personal note with the patient can never be more important' (Tasker 2019, p. 19). Research is also being presented on 'micro-robots [that] can crawl through blood vessels of the human brain'. It is 'the smallest robot yet to carry its own computer circuitry' and it offers potential breakthroughs in treating 'cancerous tumours' (The Dominion Post 2019, p. B3).

Conclusion: an industry at risk?

There seems to be a number of themes that emerge when considering not just the machines, platforms, applications and the innovations that have given a sense of urgency to an industry already noted for its rapid changing shape as, innovations continue to tumble over each other, to get into the market place first, to offer users another distraction in an age that may well be defined as distracting. These themes now appear to embrace the whole technology industry which is beginning to turn itself inside out, as it thinks about redefining its values, the role for privacy, ethics and sustainability leading to question how they should act, whether the industry needs better regulation, in what has become, at times, an unruly market place.

These themes include the need for (a) *strategic dialogue*; 'helping [us] to actively shape the world in line with common human values' (Schwab 2018b, p. x). This includes the idea about 'the need for human beings to remain central to any new digital interests or perspectives' (Watson 2018, p. xv) and not forgetting that 'we are not powerless to shape the future' (Salmon 2019, p. 4); we can make choices. Many of the authors cited write to 'stimulate thinking' so we can all 'participate in some of the major conversations of our time' (Harari 2018, p. x). (b) *The sense that regulation must come*; Sir Tim Berners-Lee writes 'Stop Web's downward plunge to dysfunctional future' adding that 'the dysfunctions harming the web' could be covered by legislation and 'systems that limit bad behaviour online', and cites his 'Contract for the Web project that he launched late last year' adding 'but initiatives like this would require all of society to contribute from members of the public to business and political leaders' (2019), Microsoft's chief legal officer and president Brad Smith suggests 'I think before one tries to say, here is the answer, one is best served by putting together a menu of options and having a conversation about them' (Fullerton 2019, p. 23). (c) *An emerging concern as to the way the industry manages itself*; 'what's needed is not more efficiency-sparkling electronics, but more human kindness and compassion' (Watson 2018, p. 3). '[A]n essential human right should be that we should be able to participate as citizens without having to do so in the digital world' (Eggers 2018, p. 28).

Although the primary message would seem to be that collaboration is the key at any level of analysis, when discussing the impact of technological innovations: from the macro level where the role of the industry itself and how it is managed is the focus to the more micro level where the relationship between humans and machines is the focus. This is closely followed by the need for new forms of leadership. While we should not underestimate the power and authority that comes with technological innovation nor should we underestimate issues like ethics, privacy, management and leadership and its sustainability and the way it shapes our lives.

Work stress research: its changing shape and direction

It is now time to take our research out onto a broader canvas acknowledging the good work that has focused on technostress (Ragu-Nathan, Tarafdar & Ragu-Nathan 2008), but begin building our research by shaping our ideas and directing our research across a wider spectrum of technological innovations to capture the way it shapes our lives. Here is a number of new and novel directions that work stress research in a digital saturated age can take: (a) explore the new meanings we should give to 'being present' in a digital age; (b) what does it mean now to be 'here and there?'; (c) exploring the merging boundaries between reality and virtual worlds and how that changes how we establish relationships and communicate. and how this reshapes the landscape of our emotional lives; (d) we should attempt to develop a measure that focuses on our 'digital everywhereness' (Scott 2016, p. 6) to capture those behaviours that are digitally dominating and shaping our lives giving us a better understanding of the changing nature of our lives and behaviours and their impact on our well-being, our relationships, and our ability to communicate all of which reflect what it is like to participate in a digital age; (e) this could be coupled with whether we engage in any counter-culture behaviours to reduce the impact of technology on our lives of such digital age behaviours, emphasizing the need to take a more mindful use of technology; (f) build on the work of Schwab (2018b) and explore the changing nature of leadership in a digital age and how leadership needs to express the values that represent 'a renaissance that is human-centred' (Schwab 2018b, p. 228); (g) exploring the nature of the synergetic relationship between people and machines by investigating what we mean by collaboration, and what we mean by establishing a relationship with a machine and understanding in more depth issues like trust, learning more about understanding technologies risks and limitations and building on, what Wilson and Daugherty (2019, p. 143), describe as 'fusion skills'; (h) then we need to explore how such relationships and collaboration are managed and what skills managers need to effectively navigate such relationships.

If our future, as Hawking describes, 'is a race between the growing power of technology and the wisdom with which we use it' (*cited in*: Shadbolt & Hampson 2018, p. 23) then a broader canvas of research may well provide a platform that better understands the relationships between people and machines allowing 'strategic dialogue' (Schwab 2018b, p. x) to take place from which wisdom may emerge.

Chapter 3

Stress and the future of work

Chapter 3 begins by exploring the multitude ways contemporary society has been described. Perhaps reinforcing the view that we live in an 'age of bewilderment' (Harari 2018, p. xiii). Not forgetting the other ways it has been described including, 'knowledge economies' or the 'weightless economy' – a 'term that has stood the test of time' (Coyle & Quah 2002, p. 8). Then there are those that capture the significance of the exponential speed and growth of technological innovation, describing our age as 'the second machine age' (Brynjolfsson & McAfee 2014), to 'the fourth industrial revolution' (Schwab 2018b). Even more descriptors capture the technological age that we live in. These include 'connectivity' and 'the age of context' (Scoble & Israel 2014) and the need to define generations as 'digital natives, and digital immigrants' (Colbert, Yee & George 2016, p. 731), not forgetting the 'internet generation' (Donkin 2010, p. 6). Moreover, perhaps, influenced by the positive psychology movement 'economies of kindness' (Ardern 2019) or 'the happiness era' (Johnson & Acabchuk 2018). All, grappling, in one way or another, with the changing nature of work – 'future work' – and the 'approaches and skills required to make the transition to more effective ways of managing people and organizing work for the overall benefit of business, individuals and society' (Maitland & Thomson 2011, p. 3).

Organizations and the nature of work in 'perpetual motion'

All these descriptors 'reveal the multiple trajectories in lived practice' (Williams 2007, p. 284). This is, as Williams argues, the direction the organization of work is taking and, more importantly, and 'unless this is recognized', then the numerous and different 'directions of change' occurring in work 'will fail to be fully understood' (Williams 2007, p. 285). As Williams goes on to argue it is 'time to shake off' the view of an 'employment-centred society' and indeed 'the dominant form of work' and so the 'employment-centred view of work needs to be challenged' (Williams 2007, pp. 285–286). Hence 'old assumptions, new work' (Ashford, George & Blatt 2007), 'the brave new workplace' (Gephart 2002), and 'what's "new" about new forms of organizing?' (Puranam, Alexy & Reitzig 2014) are all 'powerful reasons why companies and managers need to think differently about people and work [as] tectonic shifts are taking place' (Maitland & Thomson 2011, p. 3).

'Change' as Ashford, George and Blatt (2007, p. 67) suggest, 'is clearly afoot'. 'We have entered a widely heralded "new age" where work [and] organizations' are experiencing significant adjustments (Gephart 2002, p. 327) forcing researchers to investigate 'what is actually going on in the sphere of life under study' (Blumer 1969, p. 39). These point us not only to evaluate our traditional views of work, but also to 'what models, theories or conceptions of meaning can help us understand changes in the meaning of the workplace and work?' (Gephart 2002, p. 328). This chapter explores the changing nature of work and discusses, in the face of these changes, what this means for how we capture the 'new' realities of work. Questioning what that means for concepts like employability (Fugate & Kinicki 2008), the skills needed for the 21st century and working lives (Kivunja 2015), life-long learning, and the sustaining of working lives (Spreitzer, Porath & Gibson 2012).

If 'employees in full-time jobs aren't the future of work' (Mulcahy 2017, p. 187) and, as there has been, 'extraordinary growth in contingent employment arrangements' (Marler, Barringer & Milkovich 2002, p. 425), terms like 'nonstandard', have been used as a means to simply provide a norm 'against which these workers contrast' (Ashford *et al.*, 2007, p. 68). As our understanding grows around the changing nature of work, so does the way we discuss it, using terms like 'contingent workers', 'alternative working arrangements' (Spreitzer *et al.*, 2017, p. 475), 'boundaryless and traditional contingent employees' (Marler *et al.*, 2002, p. 425) and, of course the Gig economy (Mulcahy 2017). All these authors acknowledge this type of 'nonstandard' work, however described, 'is here to stay' and 'firmly rooted in the new world of work' (Spreitzer *et al.*, 2017, p. 475) and, as Gephart (2002, p. 328) correctly predicts, 'in the future' the term 'new' will simply be dropped because these alternative ways of working will establish themselves as contemporary working arrangements. So now we need to explore what employment arrangements best express the realities of working in the new millennium.

In general, two themes emerge that capture the nature of this millennium working style. These themes are: (a) 'flexibility, feasibility, the nature of the work performed, technology and changing worker preferences' (Ashford *et al.*, 2007, pp. 76–79). Others point to the importance of flexibility; 'flexibility in the employment relationship, flexibility in the scheduling of work and flexibility in where work is accomplished' (Spreitzer *et al.*, 2017, p. 473). As Mulcahy points out 'where once were *jobs*, there is increasingly just *work*' (2017, p. 6). The consequences of these changes to work means that 'people will have more jobs during their careers, and more careers during their working lives', and 'individuals will rely more heavily on marketing their unique skills, reputation and "personal brand"' (Maitland & Thomson 2011, p. 152). This means that these changes 'have enormous implications about how we think about managing our careers and structuring our lives' (Mulcahy 2017, p. 3). Not forgetting the implications for theory, our models and measures, and our discipline as the context and reality of working lives is significantly changed. This also means that we need to think about how we sustain working lives (Hirsch 2005) and sustain organizations (Pfeffer 2010).

Broader contextual changes and their influence in how work is defined

However, the working context is changing in other ways, since organizations and working lives are in 'perpetual motion' (Baruch & Hind 1999, p. 295). This chapter touches on other contextual changes including the refinement of capitalism, suggested by emphasizing 'compassionate capitalism' with its focus on individual flourishing (Myers 2007), and 'responsible capitalism' which has the aim of bringing organizations and communities closer together through developing a 'strong[er] sense of place' and a 'more collaborate ethos' (Stears & Parker 2012, pp. 3–8). 'Progressive capitalism' (Stiglitz 2019, p. 15) emphasizing 'inequalities and the common good'. Not forgetting the globalization of the concept of well-being and the ideas that GNP now needs to be re-defined to include issues like well-being and those aspects that reflect values and issues that shape the quality of life, giving a greater sense as a measure of social progress, and giving GNP a sense of those 'aspects of life that matter to people' (OECD 2013, p. 2; Stiglitz, Sen & Fitoussi 2009). The chapter ends by exploring what these changes mean for work stress. Pointing to the crucial role that context plays in our understanding of the stress process, illustrating the importance of refining measures, particularly stressors, by examining their relevance to the realities of working life. Including the direction that research needs to take to ensure our moral responsibilities are met to those whose working lives we investigate.

The context that points to why working arrangements are changing

We begin with a review of the context that aids our understanding of why work arrangements are changing. Marler and her colleagues (2002) capture several trends, although they add there are 'competing views'. The trends include, the rise of 'boundarylessness career strategies', the significance of 'intermediary institutions', the emphasis on concepts like employability, the demand for flexibility, 'out-sourcing and partnering', new technologies, and 'an increasingly diverse work force' (2002, pp. 426; 428). Gephart (2002, p. 327) argues that the commonly accepted features 'of the "business model" that dominates organizational thinking is changing' suggesting that 'contracts rather than hierarchies' are becoming indispensable organizing techniques. Maitland and Thomson add that 'connectivity' is crucial, not aiding 'a revolution in working practices in the next decade' (2011, p. 148). Smith (2002) argues, 'that uncertainty and unpredictability and to varying degrees personal risk' have 'diffused into a broad range of post-industrial workplaces' going on to add 'all three are pervasive and consistent factors shaping how people view their jobs' and 'what they experience when working' (pp. 7; 8).

In answering the question of 'why the rise in nonstandard work', Ashford and her colleagues (2007, p. 76) point to 'strategic decisions of organizations, the changing nature of work, and changing workers preferences'. All this means we must take 'a more nuanced understanding of temporary work' and recognize that this work 'has many faces' and offers 'a range of experiences' (Rogers 2000, p. 2). There is a sense that Cappelli and Keller would also offer support for a more nuanced view when they conclude that there is 'the continuing need for more detailed, fine-grained studies' (2013, p. 898). These changes may be responsible for why the economy is now being described as flexible or simply new.

From temporary, contingent employment arrangements to nonstandard work, through to the Gig economy

While this section may seem like nothing more than a simple list of changing definitions that express the evolving nature of future work, it is not just that sort of list. Its significance lies in the fact that a closer examination reveals a growing understanding of the changing nature of future work, and a sophistication in our knowledge of the structure of future work, including 'the complexity of work and employment' as we move into this millennium (Smith 2002, p. 6). It also includes the importance of the context that shapes future work, and the 'extraordinary growth' in changing 'employment arrangements' (Marler *et al.*, 2002, p. 245).

Traditional contingent employees and boundaryless workers

Two of the 'many faces' of temporary work arrangements are investigated by Marler and her colleagues (2002) – through the lens of 'traditional contingent employees and boundaryless'. These authors held that 'those who prefer boundaryless careers are an emerging group different from our traditional notion of temporary workers because they perceive their careers differently' (p. 431). What distinguishes the boundaryless workers, their research showed, was their 'preference for temporary work', the opportunity to use their skills which are marketable and needed, and which builds their knowledge and grows their experience (2002, p. 447). Another avenue to explore in terms of boundaryless workers, these authors suggest, is that they seem to have a greater acceptance 'of boundaryless careers and the notion of employability over long term-careers within one organization' (2002, p. 448). These authors also suggest there are challenges in the management of temporary workers, not just in the terms of the different types but also in their best fit with human resource strategies. Nevertheless, this study points to the complexities and challenges when identifying the different types of temporary work but offers boundaryless workers as, perhaps, an example of the flexible and new economy, and how these economies are changing the structure of employment arrangements to meet the aspirations of those who work within them.

Nonstandard work

Another 'face' of temporary work arrangements is the use of the term nonstandard work (Ashford *et al.*, 2007). Nonstandard work is distinctly different from standard work and the term is used to differentiate this type of working from the norm of standard work. It is work that is somewhat irregular and/or not permanent, and so is substantially different from traditional 9 to 5 employment. Understanding nonstandard working 'highlights the need for theories that are pertinent to their experiences and behaviours' but noting that nonstandard is a 'socially constructive' term and 'changes over time, as norms about' working arrangements alter (Ashford *et al.*, 2007, pp. 68; 74). To better understand nonstandard work, Ashford and colleagues suggest we should view it through the experiences of nonstandard working 'as existing research does not offer a nuanced or adequate understanding of the new world of work' (2007, p. 79).

These experiences (Ashford *et al.*, 2007, pp. 80; 82) include the 'freedom, autonomy and liberation from corporate control', 'the experience of boundaries' and 'the experience of relationships' – in what is becoming 'a complex social world where nonstandard and standard employees work alongside' each other and 'workers work where their families live'. These authors (*see* Ashford *et al.*, 2007, pp. 80–85) also point to a need to understand the essence of the experience directing attention to issues like how nonstandard workers cope with their role, how they handle their careers, how they deal with their new identity and what choices they had to make. What is clear these authors argue is that research should continue to focus on the experiences of nonstandard workers, as it is through this pathway that gives a better understanding of these working arrangements? Providing us with a context that aligns with the realities of this type of working, not forgetting the challenges of managing a blended workforce (Ashford *et al.*, 2007).

Temporariness and risk

Smith (2002), also argues, that the need is critical to explore temporariness when faced with a significantly changing workplace to 'look at these changes and arrangements through the eyes of the workers participating in them'. Her work expresses the 'journey' workers are taking to obtain the skills, 'the know-how', growing their 'human capital' and the resilience 'to reap the benefits of the new economy'. They must also learn 'how to map' this new employment terrain, to understand the rules and opportunities to 'cross the divide to the new era' (p. 4). In this new economy 'opportunity and advancement are intertwined with temporariness and risk' nevertheless 'workers are willing' to cope with 'the uncertainty because they felt they were gaining skills and insights that would allow them to maintain a solid footing in the new economy' (2002, pp. 7; 9). It is work that should be invested in 'rather than the pursuit of jobs' and workers should shoulder sole 'responsibility for their economic and social well-being' (2002, p. 178).

Transition from jobs to work

'Work will become more of a tradable commodity, rather than a job.' It is an era shifting for some 'from employment to deployment'. 'Work status will change. From being defined by job, organization and place in the hierarchy, it will increasingly be about a person's skills, reputation and ability to contribute and build networks' (Maitland & Thomson 2011, pp. 149; 153). The transformation of the workplace and working lives means that our research needs to go beyond just the restructuring of working lives despite its significance, requiring us to acknowledge 'that some of our most dearly held assumptions are misplaced and that we will be required to make some fundamental shifts in how we think and act our way into our future working lives' (Gratton 2014, p. 19). It means that we need to know more about how people experience working in this new economy. In addition, exploring what learning and training is needed, what skills are needed and how they transfer across working lives; how, (and how often) we may need to reinvent ourselves and 'to think about the type of working life to which we aspire' (Gratton 2014, p. 18). This means that we should refine what we understand by employability. To emphasis and reinforce these points it is time to turn our attention to and explore what has become known as the Gig economy.

The Gig economy

Mulcahy describes the Gig economy as 'still in the early stages of disrupting how we work' (2017, p. 2). Nevertheless, nonstandard work however described 'is here to stay' and 'firmly rooted in the new world of work' (Spreitzer *et al.*, 2017, p. 475). There is, notes Torres, 'no denying the growth of the gig economy' (2018, p. 146). Mulcahy makes a powerful case for the authority and significance of the Gig economy. The common theme that runs through her work is her

distinction between work and jobs. Through this distinction, she illustrates the very nature and power of the Gig economy as it is 'a new way
of working' that has 'enormous implications about how we think about
managing our careers and structuring our lives'. Since the Gig economy
carries the expectation 'to change not only the way we work but also
the way we live'. In the 'Gig Economy, where once there were *jobs*,
there is increasingly just *work*'. Put simply the Gig Economy is 'an
economy of work' (2017, pp. 3; 6; 11). Kessler also emphasizes this
distinction when she subtitles her book as 'the end of the job and the
future of work' (2019).

Maitland and Thomson, as noted above, describe work 'as [becom-
ing the] tradable commodity rather than a job' illustrating how 'contractors and consultants will bid for work online' and 'how the power
[and reach] of the Internet to allocate tasks to people anywhere in the
world by issuing a request for work'. (2011, p. 149). Similarly, Donkin
would sympathize with this view 'that organizing work into packages
called jobs is failing to meet the demands of swiftly changing businesses' (2010, p. 249). 'In the Gig Economy' Mulcahy suggests that if
'we can simply remove the rigid framework of a *job* and instead talk
about how to encourage an economy of *good work*, no matter how it is
organized and structured'. She adds 'if we can accept that the future of
work is based on work not jobs, we can start changing policies to give
workers benefits, protections and rights no matter how much or how
they work' (2017, p. 198).

Experiencing the Gig economy

Research needs to focus on the experiences of those who work in the
Gig economy. This will provide us with an understanding of such
working arrangements, giving us a context that aligns with the realities
of this work. Why? Because 'it will play an important role in exemplifying what that future might look like, and the slow, hard work that we
must do to prepare for it' (Kessler 2019, p. 250). While this literature is
a growing one, there is still a sense that our understanding of this
experience will be complex as this work has 'many faces'. It transforms
what we mean by being employed. Since we will need to generate
knowledge on what supports and learning will need to be developed to
make this work achievable, and perhaps sustainable, and what are the
attributes to operate successfully. All this is a fundamentally different
experience from the traditional ways we are acculturated to what work
means and how to go about it. Nevertheless, we can glean a sense of

how that experience is expressed when viewed through the lens of what it takes to 'thrive in the gig economy' (Petriglieri, Ashford & Wrzesniewski 2018, p. 140).

Petriglieri and his colleagues explore what 'learn[ing] it takes to be successful' as a gig worker. They acknowledge that even so, their sample, 'felt a host of social and economic anxieties without the cover and support of a traditional employer'. However, the 'independence they experienced was [their] choice and they would not give up the benefits that came with it' ... this feeling was reinforced through the 'courage they had mustered' and the more enriched lives they were leading 'than their corporate counterparts' (2018, p. 140). Working successfully in the Gig economy for their sample required strategies that 'cultivate[d] four types of connections – to *place, routines, purpose, and people*' (2018, p. 141) to survive the ups and downs of this work and to develop the 'energy and inspiration from their freedom'. Productivity is the key, helped by the fact that they can select their work that best fits their skills and aptitude with one participant summed this up by saying 'I can be the most I've ever been myself in any job' (2018, p. 141).

The reason for their success is that they 'create an environment' by setting up and nurturing what can be called described 'as liberating connections' (Petriglieri *et al.*, 2018, p. 141) The first connection 'place' where they are free from 'outside distractions' and where they are 'dedicated to work' (2018, p. 142). The second connection is 'routines' designed to boost focus and productivity, keeping to schedules and extending these routines to individual concerns and being disciplined. The third is 'purpose' giving their work a sense of a wider purpose motivated by 'serving the people I am here to serve' (2018, p. 143). The final connection is 'people' whom they can 'turn to for reassurance and encouragement' and give support that encourages them 'to take the risk' which this work necessarily involves (2018, p. 143). Again, as this work challenges traditional notions, so it does, as the authors indicate, change the meaning of success 'to a different kind of success' (2018, p. 143). Finally, the authors remind us that the risks of 'independent work are "enormously high" both in terms of financial "but also existentially"' (2018, p. 141).

Kessler's book (2019) 'gigged' turning a noun into a verb, takes us on a journey that points to the risks that are entailed, but also to the transformational nature of the journey that gig work offers through its philosophy of 'independence, flexibility, and freedom' (p. 19). Whilst still evolving and challenging the traditional structures of the labour market necessarily means that we refine what we mean by employment, the resources that gig workers need, to the very nature of work itself, giving us the need to find a new term to describe this way of working. Hence the new term, 'freelance' (Kessler 2019, p. 23). If when discussing the Gig economy in any sense 'you could reliably expect that the response would focus on flexibility' as 'the 9-to-5 job had become increasingly unrealistic for workers' (Kessler 2019, p. 59). 'It is liv[ing] the flexible … life-style.' Delivering flexibility requires that it is necessarily to surround it with the right 'support structures' (2019, pp. 236; 248). For those who work in the Gig economy 'it just means "flexibility and freedom"' (2019, p. 99). While it seems correct to assume 'that traditional employment opportunities are not what they used to be' the Gig economy 'will play an important role in exemplifying what the future might look like', and the measured, and testing effort that we must put in to get ready for it (Kessler 2019, pp. 132; 250).

Some of that 'slow, hard work' Kessler suggests, means that gig work requires the refining of what we mean by employment. The need to redefine or reclassify it is simply because gig work represents how 'a third category of workers [now] exists' (2019, p. 195). Indeed, 'the idea of creating a new category in the United States [has] gained some support' (2019, p. 195). There are still the questions about rates of pay that is challenging the Gig economy, prompting discussion of the need, perhaps, for a debate around a Universal Basic Income (Kessler 2019; Spreitzer *et al.*, 2017; Torres 2018; Watson 2018). There is also the need to explore what support structures need to be developed to aid gig workers (Kessler 2019), and coupled with this the availability of life-long learning to maintain or give the skills and prepare workers for the demands of gig work.

Two other issues shadow the Gig economy: the first is that it neces-sarily butts against traditional labour structures creating a consistent tension for significant change. Second, the trade-offs required for many create considerable emotional and social change and 'existential anxi-eties', but for those that thrive, such change and anxieties are the source of 'energy and inspiration from their freedom' (Petriglieri *et al.*, 2018, p. 141). It is clear that risks are considerable but what is clear is that the idea of 'good work' makes a difference. Kessler gives the example of the positive benefits that followed for one gig organization when they adopted a philosophy of 'not just hire them … but train them well and pay them better' (2019, p. 134). For those who succeed, their comments sum up the potential of gig working 'I don't know that I would frame [my new life] as precarious anymore … I would frame it as really living' (Petriglieri *et al.*, 2018, p. 143).

Legislation for the new (Gig) economy

A growing and expanding literature explores the employment rights of gig workers and the new economy. This literature and Government's actions are important as 'in a permanently turbulent system, we need frameworks that can usefully analyse the changing employment relationship and its consequences for both employer and employee'. (Guest 2004, p. 543). Guest explores the psychological contract as 'a useful framework' to investigate the nature of employment relations particularly when its scope is broadened to include 'issues like fairness and trust that lie at the heart of employment relations' (2004, pp. 543; 541). Healy and his colleagues suggest (Healy, Nicholson & Pekarek 2017, p. 244), that employment relations researchers can offer a meaningful input by 'mov[ing] beyond' the debate that characterizes the 'gig economy as exclusively good or bad' by asking 'under what conditions – and for whom – might gig work be beneficial?' These authors go on to conclude that 'the gig economy challenges us to re-examine what "decent work" means in the 21st century and recommit to achieving it universally' (Healy *et al.*, 2017, p. 244).

The Government in the UK has introduced 'what it claims to be the biggest package of workplace reforms for 20 years' (Syal & Stewart 2018, p. 2/6). This package stemmed from a review of modern working practices (Taylor 2017) and is built around the UK Government's commitment to legislate to improve employment status tests to 'reflect the reality of the modern working relationships' (Syal & Stewart 2018, p. 3/6), although no legislation was introduced for those on zero-hours contracts. As Guest summarizes, 'there has been growing interest in, and concern about flexible employment contract[s], culminating in European-wide legislation intended to ensure that those on such contracts are not treated less favourably than those in permanent employment' (Guest 2004a, p. 5). The 'EU uses the term "flexicurity" to denote labour market flexibility combined with worker protection' (Maitland & Thomson 2011, p. 151). It seems that the term employment now needs to be refined, by exploring the nature 'of [employment] arrangements' to refine what being employed now means when working in the Gig economy (Flanagan 2017, p. 380). 'Our labour market needs to reflect that work in the Gig economy doesn't always, or even mostly, take place in a job' (Mulcahy 2017, p. 199).

Skills and learning that fit the new economy

We begin by setting a probable context to explore the idea of what skills and learning are needed at a time when the skills needed 'to keep up in any job are churning at a [fast] rate' (Selingo & Simon 2017, p. 1/5). Maitland and Thomson (2011, pp. 152–154) paint a picture where careers are changing shape and 'will be become more fluid and less linear or ladder shaped' where 'individuals will rely more heavily on marketing their unique skills, reputation and "personal brand"'. 'Hierarchical thinking' will need to change with 'organizational cultures learn[ing] to separate status from hierarchy' and workers will be 'asking more searching questions about why we work the way that we do'. These are the beginning signs of how work is transforming rather than just changing. It is, as Gratton suggests (2014, p. 196), as the pace of this transformation quickens 'what will go are many of the beliefs about what work is and how it is performed'. It is also important to remember that training, retraining and learning will 'not be one offs' as technology has the power to represent 'a cascade of ever-bigger disruptions'. '[We] will need the ability to constantly learn and to reinvent [ourselves]' (Harari 2018, pp. 32; 265).

Looking at the specific skills needed carries with it, a difficulty: because we don't know what future work may look like, 'we don't really know what particular skills people will need' (Harari 2018, p. 262). What, perhaps, we do know is how people should prepare for the future. That is by learning to learn through participating in lifelong learning as we emphasize again we will need the ability to constantly learn and to retransition ourselves. Nevertheless, 'many pedagogical experts' point to the importance of teaching 'the 4Cs': 'critical thinking, communication, collaboration and creativity' (*see* Harari 2018, pp. 265; 262). Similarly, creative and social skill follows from the work of Frey and Osborne (2013, p. 45) and while Watson 'endorse [these]' skills he adds 'empathy, intuition, nuance and personality' (2018, p. 188). Again, Kivunja (2015, pp. 2; 3), offers a 'Domain of the New Learning Paradigm' which includes a component describing 'Career and Life skills' which cover skills like, 'flexibility and adaptability, Initiative and self-direction, social and cross-cultural, productivity and accountability and leadership and responsibility'. Gratton adds (2014, p. 18) that it is skills like 'connectivity, collaboration and networking' that 'will be central'. What is interesting about the skills we have been discussing is, it feels like these skills are not yet part of the repertoire of learning machines or robotics and they 'help us discuss what it means to be human' (Watson 2018, p. 189). Are these skills put forward to meet the changes of future work, simply saying do not forget the value of being human?

Ansell (2016, p. 2) ends her piece on 'bring on lifelong learning' by drawing attention to how lifelong learning 'makes it possible [to] be more resilient to the ups and downs of the modern labour market' and asking us to recognize 'that jobs are no longer for life and education is not just for the young'. Selingo and Simon (2017, p. 4/5) express similar sentiments when they discuss the potential of what they describe as 'renewable learning'. '[It] is no longer a nice to have, but a need to have for employees and employers to succeed in today's rapidly evolving world of work.' While it may require some universities and colleges to look at how they provide lifelong learning there is no doubting its potential, its authority and power. The skill of learning to learn is given to us by lifelong learning. The Government of the UK has acknowledged its significance and 'is considering whether the time is right to look again at "lifetime learning support"' (Ansell 2016, p. 1) recognizing the power of lifelong learning through the idea of a proposed lifelong learning allowance.

Interestingly, Harari (2018, p. 35) foreshadowed this moment when he wrote that, 'Governments will have to step in, both by subsidising a lifelong education sector and by providing a safety net for the inevitable periods of transition.' There is a sense in Gratton's writing (2014, p. 200) that it is lifelong learning that aids the 'regeneration' process that contemporary working requires when individuals think 'about the type of working life to which [they] aspire' and 'the trade offs' they may have to make (Gratton 2014, p. 18). As it seems that lifelong learning gives, not just a sense of resilience but it also fortifies and 'builds depth' in terms of a person's intellectual capital that is 'a combination of what you know and your capacity to think deeply and intelligently about issues and challenges'. Lifelong learning builds intellectual capital by increasing 'cognitive capacity and the depth of learning'. 'It is clear', argues Gratton (pp. 199; 198), 'that in the future intellectual capital will become increasingly important in the creation of valuable jobs and careers'.

Technology's impact on work and jobs

This is, as mentioned in Chapter 2, the 'will it, won't it' question and 'will only be answered with hindsight' (Watson 2018, p. 176). However, there are a number of ways this question can be approached.

The first is exploring the different 'categories' of technology and their impact on jobs, the second 'a major focus of research and public concern' is what jobs will be replaced by technology (Chui, Manyika & Miremadi 2016, p. 1/14), and the third is more an exploration of the potential of technology and the different scenarios that may emerge. These three options are not mutually exclusive as each colours the other, but each gives insights into whether we can, or how far we can go, in answering the 'will it, won't it' question raised by Watson (2018). We briefly explore each approach.

Approach I: distinguishing between types of technology

Calling on the work of economists, Salmon, indicates that 'distinguishing between types of innovation with different impacts is increasingly common' (2019, p. 18). Salmon turns to the work of Christensen and van Bever (2014, p. 60) who identify three types of innovation (technology). These they describe as (a) 'performance-improving' 'which replace old products with better models'; (b) 'efficiency innovations – which lower costs, don't produce many jobs (indeed they eliminate them)' and (c) 'market-creating innovations; which transform products so radically they create a new class of consumer, – do generate jobs for their originators and for the economy'. 'Why bother with such distinctions? Because when it comes to their direct impact on jobs, these three types of innovation differ greatly' (Salmon 2019, p. 16).

Salmon (2019), also calls on the work of the Nobel Prize winning economist Acemoglu who also offers a classification scheme (*see review*: by Bawagan of Acemoglu 2017). There 'are [Acemoglu suggests] two types', 'replacing and enabling technologies – and this distinction is important' (Acemoglu 2017, p. 2/5). He goes on to explain that replacing technologies – 'replace workers but they don't reduce your costs all that much. If that's the case you lose the workers in the displacement effect, but the productivity effect doesn't change' (p. 2/5). 'Enabling technologies like robotics and AI should translate to increased productivity and wages, but we haven't seen it yet'. The 'basic lesson is clear: the potential of technology can only be fully and equitably realized with a range of other complementary investments' (p. 3/5). Perhaps Acemoglu (2017) was thinking about skills training and learning and collaborating skills as they may reflect such 'complementary investments', as he goes on to say 'more research is needed to guide policies on what skills are important and how organizations and education systems must adapt' (p. 3/5). 'We are', he concludes 'really very much in the middle of some very transformative changes' (p. 3/5). Salmon ends his discussion on the categories of technology approach and sees its power 'as [it] can help us see more clearly what is happening amid the technological hype today' (2019, p. 21).

Approach II: the impact of technology on jobs and work

The second option is to explore the impact of technology on jobs. This too requires a nuanced approach. It is necessary, argue Chui and colleagues, to understand the factors that influence automation potential. These factors set a context when thinking about the automation of work. The first factor (a) requires, when thinking about work, that it is important to remember that different tasks in that work will have 'varying degrees of technical feasibility' (Chui *et al.*, 2016, p. 2/14). A number of other factors help to create a context that illustrates the complexities of decisions to automate. These include: (b) research and development costs; (c) labour costs and it's supply and demand; (d) other factors that go beyond just worker replacement issues and focus on issues surrounding the potential improvements in the quality of performance and; (e) 'regulatory and social-acceptance factors ... must also be weighed' (*see* Chui *et al.*, 2016, p. 4/14). Also important to understand when automation occurs is 'this does not necessarily spell the end of the jobs in that line of work'. These factors simply create a context that represents a delicate interaction between them 'and the trade-offs among them' (p. 4/14).

Chui and his colleagues then begin by exploring what work has the highest level of 'technical feasibility of automating work activities' (p. 3). This work includes, in no order of feasibility: (a) manufacturing, food service, accommodations and retailing. This list does not capture the nuanced approach of the authors (Chui *et al.*, 2016) as they show how in each category of work there will be different activities against which automation levels will vary remembering that 'just because an activity can be automated doesn't mean that it will be – broader economic factors are at play' (p. 6/14). Work 'in the middle range for automation' (9/14) also carries the nuances, and subtleness of their analysis. This category includes (b) financial services and insurance where around the majority 'of the overall time of the workforce is devoted to collecting and processing data' ... similarly 'with the financial sector where the technical potential to automate 'activities taking up [almost half] of its workers' time' (p. 9/14). Other work in this 'middle range' where workplaces 'are unpredictable and where flexibility is demanded' like farming, forestry and construction 'are for now more difficult to automate with current demonstrated technology', although in each industry there are activities that 'are more susceptible to automation' (p. 10/14).

Finally, Chui and his colleagues point to that work which has low technical potential for automation. This work includes (c) those involved in dealing 'and developing people or that apply expertise to decision making, planning, or creative work' (2016, p. 10/14). The significance of personal interplay is manifest 'in two sectors that, so far, have a relatively low potential for automation: healthcare and education'. This is 'at least for now' (p. 11/14). Again, it depends on who does what within these professions. It is, as Chui and his colleagues note (2016, p. 12/14), that purely focusing on 'the technical potential for automation' is not sufficient to judge 'how much of it will occur in particular activities'. 'It is', as they point out (Chui *et al.*, 2016, p. 13/14), 'never too early to prepare for the future', leadership is required as is the need to understand the opportunities and rethink 'how workers engage with their jobs and how digital labour platforms can better connect individuals, teams and projects' (13/14). A sense perhaps, that at the heart of the automation debate is the synergetic relationship between the machine and humans, and perhaps this represents another factor to add to this already complex context, the key for success may lie in through the way machines and humans collaborate.

The work by Frey and Osborne (2013) is also a work of nuanced complexity and thoughtfulness. They make it clear that they are not predicting the future or trying to calculate 'future changes' in the way work and the labour market is reconfigured (2013, p. 36). They find that high probability industries (transportation and logistics, office and administrative support workers, services, sales and labour construction occupations), followed by a medium risk category (installation, maintenance and repair occupations) but in this group 'incremental technological improvements' may reduce the 'comparative advantage of human labour' (2013, p. 39). In the low risk category ('in short, generalist occupations requiring knowledge of human heuristics' and those 'involving the develop of novel ideas and artefacts, including management, education, healthcare as well as arts and media jobs)' (2013, p. 40). So, a variety of tasks 'involving social intelligence are unlikely to become subject to computerisation in the near future' (2013, p. 41).

This brief summary cannot capture the depth of analysis and the complexity, and nuances of Frey and Osborne's work. They make it clear (Frey & Osborne 2013, p. 42), they are not trying to make any estimates as to 'how many jobs will actually be automated'. They too, point to how contextual factors make it particularly problematic to make 'any predictions about technological progress' (p. 43). Complicating classifying jobs is that 'waves of computerization' will occur, 'separated by' what Frey and Osborne describe as a 'technological plateau' (2013, p. 38). Other contextual factors include 'future wage levels, capital prices or labour shortages', then regulation anxieties and 'political activism' and the need to 'focus on near-term technological breakthroughs' (p. 43). For workers though, the message is clear 'they will have to acquire creative and social skills' (p. 45).

Approach III: the exploration of the potential of technology

This is more of a contextual approach, exploring the potential relationship that develops between machines and workers. So, as Watson (2018, pp. 172; 173) suggests, 'how technology changes work is critical' and adds that an 'underappreciated aspect' of this, is the way that 'the machines themselves are changing'. It is clear that we are at a transformational point and yet this is 'merely the beginning'. Nevertheless, as Watson mentions (2018, p. 181), the fact that work can be automated 'doesn't necessarily mean it has to be' and the question that needs to be asked is; what else 'we might do to make work people-centric in an age of machines?' It points, Harari (2018, p. 29) argues, to the fundamental importance of defining the relationship in terms of collaboration and cooperation 'rather than competition' between the two.

The upheaval will be significant and no work 'will ever be safe from the threat of future automation, because machine learning and robotics will continue to improve' (Harari 2018, p. 30). Yet some changes may nevertheless be 'blocked' by politicians and consumers (Harari 2018, p. 33) because they are viewed as socially unacceptable, and, as Harari (2018, p. 32) wonders, whether people 'will have the emotional stamina necessary for a life of such endless upheavals'. There is also the question, posed by Harari (2018, p. 29), that it may become 'easier' to 'create new jobs than retraining [workers] to actually fill these jobs'. Perhaps we should keep reminding ourselves that 'the real value of work is not what we produce for others, but what work produces in ourselves' (Watson 2018, p. 187). In a time of transformation, it is good work that motivates that transformation in each of us. If we are living in an 'age of bewilderment' as Harari suggests (2018, p. xiii), we may well be, somewhat bewildered, 'between wondering what the new world will bring and living it' (Dewe & Cooper 2017, p. 34).

More changing contours of the work context

Sustainability

While well-being has always played a central role in our discipline, a number of trends have returned our focus to its primary role. Now the focus is on individuals thriving through work that is sustaining. The work on human capital through its sustaining and development properties and the growing body of work on what good work means are examples of this. The subtleness of this approach lies in its focus on individual workers their development and in many respects their thriving (Spreitzer, Porath & Gibson 2012). It is taking us back to our roots and to our primary role where we are principally 'concern[ed] for the well-being of the individual worker' and our 'humanist tradition' (Lefkowitz 2011, p. 114; 2008, p. 444). To support this focus we first, explore the question of how can working lives be made more sustainable? The topic of sustainability and its accompanying research interest points to the difference between ecological sustainability and social sustainability. As we have noted before (Dewe & Cooper 2017), Pfeffer makes the case for the latter by arguing that 'it is not just the natural world that is at risk from harmful business practices. We should care as much about people' adding that this means our focus should be on these practices in order to 'understand [their] causes and consequences and [direct] our research attention towards them' (2010, p. 43). This focus explores how can we make working lives more sustainable and offer workers the opportunity to have a 'more productive, balanced and fulfilling role' (Dewe & Cooper 2017, p. 38; Hirsch 2005; Spreitzer *et al.*, 2012). Sustaining work provides a sense of individual development, and growth, resilience, relevance and satisfaction. In this way, this work experience provides individuals with the means to meet the challenges of the new economy. Its value can be seen as a package of measures that enhance the quality of working lives.

Human capital

The second trend points to the growing interest in human capital as a resource and how it can be expressed and measured to illustrate it value, and its potential. Its emphasis is on growth and development. It is 'the most valuable resource in business' (Spreitzer, Porath & Gibson 2012, p. 161). This work now embraces human (intellectual) capital – (what you know), social capital (who you know), (Luthans *et al.*, 2007, p. 20; Dewe & Cooper 2017, p. 73) and more recently psychological capital as it focuses on 'who you are', with an emphasis on growth and development through 'who you are becoming' (Luthans *et al.*, 2007, p. 20). Not forgetting emotional capital ('understanding yourself and being reflexive'), 'intellectual capital' (Gratton 2014, pp. 198–200) or 'the new human capital equation' (Cascio 2007, p. 15).

These views see human capital as a resource and more particularly, point to how it can be nurtured, developed and maintained by the work you choose, giving you the capacity to 'differentiate yourself, reconcile your emotional needs' (Gratton 2014, pp. 199; 201) and for all to monitor, and measure their health, wellness and well-being (Roslender, Stevenson & Kahn 2006).

The meaning of good work

The third trend looks at the meaning of good work. As we have discussed before (Dewe & Cooper 2017, p. 83) 'the good work agenda' builds from the proposal that work 'engages all our skills, talents, capabilities and emotions' (Coats & Lekhi 2008, p. 13; Dewe & Cooper 2017, p. 83). 'It is, work that is good work, is the only work that is good for us' (Coats 2009, p. 10). When thinking what good work actually means, then good work is expressed in terms that captures what we have been discussing above in the other two trends. It is good health (Black 2008), growth, development, positive and motivated behaviours and the opportunity to use talents and skills (Constable, Coats, Bevan & Mahdon 2009). It provides a sense of meaningfulness, fulfilment, self-esteem and a life of value (Brown, Charlwood, Forde & Spencer 2006; Dewe & Cooper 2017, p. 83; Overall 2008; Parker & Bevan 2011). The aim is to translate this work by giving meaning to good work into policy to see it fulfil its promise and initiate 'tangible change in the workplace' (Constable *et al.*, 2009, p. 7; Dewe & Cooper 2017, p. 83). These three trends in organization psychology capture our humanistic base and give us an opportunity and motivation to use this knowledge, and its aims and objects. To begin to explore the experience of working in the new economy, to focus on the meaning of work as distinct from jobs, and to explore how collaboration, trust and technology matches with these aspirations.

Future directions for research

As this chapter illustrates, we will need to adopt a broad canvas around 'future work' when focusing on the future directions for research. A number of avenues emerge from this chapter. They include

a   Probing the distinction between work and jobs. This distinction has a number of perspectives. The first is to identify the structure of jobs and identify the significant features that distinguish jobs from those parameters that define the meaning of work. Our research has focused primarily on jobs, their characteristics and motivational potential. That needs to change as Mulcahy (2017, p. 189) reinforces 'as stick[ing] stubbornly to an old outdated model that defines "jobs" and "employees" in ways that are increasingly irrelevant and obstruct innovation, growth, and opportunity'. Other issues flow from this:

b   The most significant one is we need to explore is the categorization of workers beyond 'employees or contractors', capturing the third category that describes what it means to be a 'freelancer' and begin to establish the boundaries of how this third category distinguishes itself from what we understand are employees and contractors. Again, not introducing a third category of workers 'creates permanent distortions and inefficiencies' in the labour market (Mulcahy 2017, p. 189).

c   This means we need to think through what we mean by employability, particularly if we have to continually redefine ourselves and consider what we mean by a career and the way it is managed, and what it means to be successful in the new economy. This, necessarily, will create a need to continue to build the work on the skills needed to work in this new economy. This in turn signals the importance of lifelong learning and considering its provision and availability as learning is now a life experience. Perhaps one skill we will need is the 'ability to transition' in an age where it too is transitioning. Perhaps we should focus more on learning rather than training – giving a perspective that is broader than the traditional training approach.

d   One way to approach these points so far is to build on the literature that focuses on how workers experience work in the Gig economy – its good and bad points – and what best defines those experiences. Exploring how they understand and give meaning to their role, their career and their new identity, what skills they need and how they transfer across working lives. Including how (and how often) there will be the need to reinvent themselves and what this means in terms of what they wish to achieve (*see* Gratton 2014). Not forgetting the choices they make. This will build a context and an explanatory platform to tackle some of the issues we have outlined above – the meaning of work, categorization, employability, the skills required and the experience of working in the Gig economy. Understanding these experiences of working in the Gig economy gives us a sense of meaning, a context for understanding how these experiences differ from those in traditional roles.

e   The research direction above will begin to align our work with the realities of future work, giving it relevance and through this person focus meet our responsibilities to those whose working lives we research and, in the end, emphasizing that humanistic core that reflects the fundamental nature of our discipline.

Chapter 4

Coping with work stress

Introduction

This chapter begins by emphasizing how fundamental our understanding of how people cope is to work stress research (Dewe & Cooper 2017), with researchers showing a 'boundless enthusiasm for' this type of research (Aldwin 2000, p. 73). This is not to suggest that empirical research on coping has been free of controversy, particularly when questions of measuring strategies are the focus of debate (Coyne & Racioppo 2000). Perhaps, coping research derives its importance to us, as researchers, simply because there is this sense of 'immediate personal relevance' (Aldwin 2000, p. 73) that comes with it. It also 'relates to the quality and the ensuing constructive meaning of our own lives' (Snyder 1999, p. 5). Coping research has emphasized the importance of being 'sensitive to the complexities [when] measuring' strategies by developing our understanding through the frameworks we derive to classify them (Dewe & Cooper 2017, p. 143).

There are six reasons that make classifying coping strategies empirically strategic. The first is that classifying strategies is described as an evolving process, as classification frameworks represents, at any one time, our state of knowledge (Folkman 2011). The second reason, qualitatively different to the first, illustrates the fundamental role that the 'context' plays when classifying coping strategies so any framework must reflect the realities of contemporary work and work behaviours. The third reason:

> is that we should always keep an eye on the social context in which our models live. If our societal values shift as we move into the next century, then coping researchers should keep their hands on the pulse of this changing society.
>
> (Snyder 1999, p. 331)

The fourth reason points to the growing interest in well-being, through the emphasis on human capital and resource-based strategies – 'competing through people' (Dewe & Cooper 2017, p. 15). The fifth reason flows from the growing 'digital fluency' of the workforce, and our developing understanding of 'cyberbehaviours' (Colbert *et al.*, 2016, p. 733). Finally, the sixth reason, in many ways, sums up all these reasons and collects them together under the rubric that it is, 'those who do research on coping increasingly are called upon to comment on a variety of events that are occurring in society' (Snyder 1999, p. 324).

At the heart of this chapter, is our focus on the role that 'cyber-behaviours' like 'cyberloafing' (Lim, Teo & Loo 2002; Lim & Chen 2012), may play in broadening our view of coping strategies and fulfil a need to explore and perhaps adopt in our classification frame-work, a coping strategy that reflects cyberbehaviours. Researchers have already, begun to explore the idea of 'redesigning work for a digital workforce' and 'leveraging' the 'mindful usage of technology in ways that promote time for focused thinking, opportunities for recovery, and effective collaborations' (Colbert *et al.*, 2016, p. 735), all perhaps expressing technologies potential role as a coping strategy. We also, in this chapter, as we have done before (Dewe & Cooper 2012; 2017), emphasize the fundamental importance of the process of primary appraisal – the meanings given to stressful encounters – in coping research and work stress generally. 'Apprais-als' are the context within which coping strategies are embedded and their explanatory power is reflected in Snyder's comment, 'I believe that it is incumbent upon each proponent of a new coping theory to explicate the nature of the appraisal process' (1999, p. 331).

The chapter also turns to the positive psychology movement (Selig-man & Csikszentmihalyi 2000), and its influence on coping research; pointing to the need to investigate the role of positive outcomes and emotions; following on from the dictum from Lazarus and Cohen-Charash that 'discrete emotions are the "coin of the realm" in coping research' (2001, p. 45). Here, we are drawn, to explore the interest in 'happiness', and its potential relationship with coping. The chapter also explores the question somewhat ignored, but frequently inferentially acknowledged, by what do we mean by 'coping effectiveness' (Dewe & Cooper 2017). The chapter concludes by taking up the issues of refinement and relevance that gives coping research its power, signifi-cance, meaning and credibility, allowing us to better understand the potential of coping research. Reinforcing how that the 'stress and the coping narrative evolves with the accumulation of research findings' (Folkman 2011, p. 461).

Classification of coping strategies

Folkman, along with colleagues, in a number of thoughtful and insightful reviews (Folkman & Moskowitz 2004; Folkman 2011; 2009), describes the evolution of coping research. It is in this context that our understanding of this 'complex, multidimensional process' and 'the diversity of conceptualizations of coping' challenges researchers to find 'a common nomenclature' for coping strategies 'so that findings across studies can be discussed meaningfully' (Folkman 2011a, p. 9; Folkman & Moskowitz 2004, pp. 747; 751). Folkman and Moskowitz nicely illustrate the evolving nature of classifying coping strategies when discussing the 'useful way' they have been classified in the past, beginning with the distinction between 'problem-focused' and 'emotion-focused' coping; a 'jumping-off point' for many studies (Folkman 2011, p. 454). While this distinction was described by Folkman and Moskowitz as a 'broad brushstrokes' approach it 'was a good starting point' (2004, pp. 751–752). As, our knowledge advanced two further categories were added – 'meaning-focused' and 'social' coping. These four categories reflected 'the now-familiar pattern' that 'helps the synthesis of findings across studies' (2004, p. 752). Later Folkman was to 'highlight' 'three major gaps in the original formulation' and 'new developments' relating to 'future orientation, religious and spiritual coping, and interpersonal coping' (2011, p. 454; Folkman & Moskowitz 2004, p. 756). It is, this context that reflects the evolving nature of coping categories, which we add the need to explore the role that 'cyberbehaviours' like cyberloafing (Lim, Teo & Loo 2002; Lim & Chen 2012) may play in expanding our view of coping strategies. The aim is to explore whether it fulfils our need to capture the realities of contemporary work, and warrants adopting a coping strategy that reflects these cyberbehaviours.

However, first a warning that creating 'a common nomenclature' for coping strategies 'runs the risk' by 'masking important differences within categories' (Folkman & Moskowitz 2004, p. 752). The irony is that classifying coping strategies, while empirically strategic, does have the potential to disguise the subtleties and complexity when exploring coping strategies in action. This involves remembering the need to think about the way in which coping strategies are actually being used, how they may work together, whether using one prevents the need to use another, and the patterns they may form and what that tells us about their relationship with one-another, their timing, and about how they are usually being used. Focusing on these issues may well help us 'so that we can learn more about how coping works' (Folkman & Moskowitz 2004, p. 754). All these issues reflect future directions researchers may wish to engage in to better understanding coping in action.

The issues noted above also raise questions about the way that we evaluate and express the psychometrics of coping categories; since individual coping strategies in a particular category may be used in ways which do not necessarily conform to the rules required to capture high levels of internal consistency (Folkman & Moskowitz 2004, pp. 752–753). Nevertheless, developing a common language through classifying coping strategies is empirically strategic because it provides a utility of interpretation and gives a commonality to measures when investigating the dynamics of the stress process offering a context within which results can be compared and explained.

Then, as noted earlier, we need to think about the influence of the positive psychology movement and acknowledge the work on the role of positive emotions, and the co-occurrence of positive and negative emotions in a stressful encounter, their role and purpose. The work on emotional avoidance and emotional approach coping, the flexibility of coping strategies and stress related growth, all, in their way, capturing the transactional nature of coping (Folkman & Moskowitz 2004).

Cyberloafing

Cyberloafing research, may well have its origins, it seems, from work that focused on the problems of frequent internet users (Stanton 2002). This work, not surprisingly, found that a more complex picture of internet use emerged pointing more towards that 'frequent internet use does not equal a diagnosis of internet addiction and that high frequency internet users may often be happy and productive workers' and 'express more positive attitudes about their organization' (Stanton 2002, pp. 58–59). This 'cast doubt on the popular profile of the workplace internet addict', suggesting further investigations around the ways the internet was being used and whether in the light of the above findings such behaviours offered other positive uses (Stanton 2002, p. 58).

To 'facilitate [this] discussion' Lim and colleagues introduced us to the term ' "cyberloafing" to refer 'to any voluntary act of employees using their companies' internet access during office hours to surf nonwork-related Web sites for nonwork purposes and access' (Lim *et al.*, 2002, p. 67). The aim of these researchers was to explore how frequently, and why, employees cyberloafed. In terms of the frequency almost a quarter 'reported they used the internet to browse nonwork-related Web sites a few times a day' whilst a similar percentage 'reported they browsed nonwork-related Web sites a few times a week'. While employees 'typically visited general news sites, or downloaded nonwork-related information, other popular destinations included entertainment, investment and sport related sites'. These activities, the authors suggest, reflect the blurring of boundaries between home and work and that 'people may simply take whatever time is available to them to engage in certain activities' (Lim *et al.*, 2002, pp. 68; 69). When exploring what drove employees to cyberloaf the comments generally suggested that 'when employees are able to rationalize their right to use their companies' internet access for nonwork purposes, they would not be averse to cyberloafing' (Lim *et al.*, 2002, p. 69).

As the interest in cyberloafing grew, Lim and Chen in a recent study outlined their aim to 'examine how and when cyberloafing can have a positive effect on work so that its potential benefits can be harnessed'. Arguing that this aim was an 'imperative [one] for scholars' stressing the need to explore the 'impact of cyberloafing on employees' work and emotions' (2012, p. 343). From their four hypotheses our focus was directed to the one that explored the 'impact of cyberloafing on employees' emotions' (2012, p. 344). Their findings 'revealed that cyberloafing generates [a] positive impact on work' by making 'work more interesting', giving support to deal with practical and work issues, made them 'a better and more interesting worker' and offered them support and help when dealing with work problems. Moreover, 'browsing activities were found to have a positive impact on employees' emotion[s]' (2012, pp. 346; 351). In their discussion the authors turned to the language of coping to explain their results, by suggesting that 'some browsing activities allow for relief from work and motivate employees to perform better' and it 'allows employees to take an innocuous break from what otherwise would be a stressful environment' (2012, pp. 351; 352). Their conclusions emphasize that cyberloafing 'is an area which warrants future research attention' as does how it should be managed in organizations to allow its benefits to be expressed (2012, p. 352).

The language of coping to explain cyberloafing has not just been confined to Lim's and Chen's (2012) work but has found its way into the work of other authors as well. There is a sense that one way to express the benefits of cyberloafing is to see it as a mechanism that 'takes you away' and relieves you for a moment from the rigours of work and so acts as a re-invigorating and energizing experience (Simmers, Anandarajan & D'Ovidio 2008; Stanton 2002). This focus reinforces the need to explore the positive ways the web can contribute to working lives (Lim & Chen 2012). We believe these researchers are sending a signal that now is the time to integrate this reality of contemporary work into coping research, capturing the 'digital fluency' of the workforce and exploring if cyberloafing marks it place as a coping strategy and an example of the 'mindful use of technology' (Colbert *et al.*, 2016, pp. 732; 735).

A brief interlude with busyness and the tyranny of productivity

This interlude is to illustrate how digital awareness and fluency, combined with technology generally, have begun to alter the meanings of concepts like being productive and busy. Offering an explanation that helps to set a context for understanding why including cyberbehaviours into coping research not just captures the realities of work but how these behaviours 'might influence the future workplace' (Colbert *et al.*, 2016, p. 731). Newport (2016, p. 64) introduces us to 'busyness' where 'if you send and answer e-mails at all hours, if you schedule and attend meetings constantly [and] weigh in on instant message systems ... all these behaviours make you seem busy in a public manner'; then this becomes the new busyness. As Colbert and her colleagues point out 'future research is needed to fully understand how digital fluency may influence job performance and career progression' offering how organizations consider 'how they "promote mindful usage" of technology' (2016, pp. 732; 735). To Newport (2016, pp. 64; 65; 66), the behaviours mentioned above 'seem crucial for convincing yourself and others that you're doing your job well ... in the increasingly bewildering psychic landscape of our daily work' but simply 'lure you away' from deep work.

In fact, Newport argues, that 'deep work is exiled in favour of more distracting high-tech behaviours' (2016, p. 69). This means researchers need to consider a context where technology influences the meanings we give to concepts, like being busy or productive by exploring the changing nature of the workplace. Illustrating a context where digital fluency can at times promote behaviours that generally act as a potential source of role overload, leading researchers to consider refining our meaning of traditional role stressors. However, technology generally, has a 'yin and yang' role – its dualism – its mindful use, nudging researchers towards thinking about its potential as offering a more supportive role, as a possible source of coping.

Watson (2018, p. 184) introduces us, to what he describes as the 'cult of productivity'. As Watson goes on to point out 'busyness, not idleness, is the badge of honour in our 24/7, machine-centric, capitalist economy' (2018, p. 185). This follows the idea as to how behaviours are influenced by technology in the workplace and sets a context that gives a new perspective to what it means to be productive in contemporary workplaces. Watson then turns his attention to this new form of busyness driven via technology and embedded in the 'cult of productivity', making it clear that it doesn't have to be like this in the workplace. Watson suggests that 'looking out of a window and thinking is generally seen as monumentally unproductive, which is monumentally nonsense' (2018, p. 185). Going on to add that 'first, we need to take a break' that 'wasted time is not time wasted' and that 'marinating your mind in magazines, or chatting to mates will be the most productive thing you do all day, because it can lead to new insights and ideas' since it is 'when our minds are unoccupied and empty that a real self-awareness occurs' (2018, pp. 185; 186).

Calling on 'a need for renewal', and the science associated with it, the conclusion is 'that we are more receptive to new ideas when our minds are allowed to wander' (Watson 2018, pp. 186; 187). It is tempting to add cyberloafing into this list of mindfulness activities, and for researchers to acknowledge the yin and yang nature of technology. Directing our future research to explore technologies potential for offering a coping strategy to counter the new busyness or indeed enhancing it by taking cyberbreaks aimed also at the flourishing growth of this new cult of productivity.

The significance of the concept of primary appraisal

In this chapter, as we have done before (Dewe & Cooper 2012; 2017), we emphasize the fundamental importance of the process of primary appraisal – the meanings given to stressful encounters – in coping research and work stress generally. The significance of 'cognitive appraisals' cannot be disputed and, why we emphasize it again here, as appraisals provide a personnel context that informs 'the quality of the individual's emotional response' to a stressful encounter and 'to the ways in which the person cope[s]' (Folkman & Moskowitz 2004, p. 746). Lazarus (2000, p. 665), when discussing his transactional theory of stress, describes the importance of the role of primary appraisal in these terms, 'The conceptual bottom line of my approach is the *relational meaning* that an individual constructs from the person-environment relationship.' Expanding on this approach Lazarus adds,

> an appraisal-centered approach to stress directs our attention not merely to environmental stressors but to how these stressors are construed by a person. I am confident that personal meanings are the most important aspects of psychological stress with which the person must cope, and they direct the choice of coping strategy.
>
> (1993, pp. 243–244)

Folkman (2009, p. 74) explains the significance of the role of appraisal in this way, 'in a model that is contextual, the key contextual variables including the stressor itself and its related appraisal, coping and emotion processes'. To ignore appraisals, is to ignore a compelling and powerful piece of the stress process and its context, not forgetting the explanatory potential that accompanies it when exploring coping. It is, as Snyder (1999, p. 331) opines, 'my sense is that we only have scratched the surface in our understanding of the contribution that appraisal plays in the coping process'. A conspicuous omission when 'the coping process is initiated in response to the individual's appraisal' (Folkman & Moskowitz 2004, p. 747). Coming, to terms with appraisals requires researchers to step from 'analysis thinking' to 'thinking in synthesis' terms, in an 'effort to reconstruct the whole so that the phenomena under study are restored to the form in which they appear in nature' (Lazarus 2000, pp. 667–668). Although, as Lazarus suggests, each approach 'complement each other, their scientific tasks are sufficiently distinctive to require different lines of thought and research methods' (2000, p. 668).

A possible first step in this process should be to elevate 'appraisal' to its central place in coping and work stress research perhaps by beginning qualitatively. Qualitative approaches are 'incredibly diverse, complex and nuanced' (Braun & Clarke 2006, p. 78). The question to be asked could be something like 'what did the stressful encounter mean to you'? Thematic analysis would organize the data in a way that allows it to be described in rich detail (Braun & Clarke 2006) offering a stronger link and a greater sensitivity to the more subtle aspects of the data. Not, altogether dissimilar, from developing a thematic map associated to the question asked (Braun & Clarke 2006). 'Detailed description', as Lazarus comments, is an important part of our science

(Lazarus 2000, p. 668). The approach, of course, is up to future researchers to decide. However, the primary context for such research is to acknowledge the subtle differences between meanings given to a stressful encounter and the nature of the stressful encounter (stressor) itself. The aim should be to provide a fundamental piece of the stress process (appraisals) that seems to have alluded work stress researchers, giving our research a more 'full and accurate *description* of phenomenal wholes' enabling synthesis to occur in our work (Lazarus 2000, p. 668).

The positive psychology of coping

It is Folkman and Moskowitz (2000, p. 647) who lead the way by reviewing what they describe as 'as the other side of the coin, an approach that examines positive affect in the stress process'. What they argue is 'an underrepresented [area] in coping research'. While they show that 'positive affect has not been entirely neglected in models of stress', difficulties still lie in the path of researchers wishing to take up this challenge. These difficulties include (*see* Folkman & Moskowitz 2000, p. 647) issues around how coping is measured, the 'underutilization of qualitative methods' and that little attention has been paid to 'the interpersonal aspects of coping'. To this list Folkman and Moskowitz add the role of positive affect in coping, and we would add, particularly in work stress research, the often-unacknowledged role of 'primary appraisal', even though there is general agreement across researchers that 'coping is influenced by the appraised characteristics of the stressful context' (Folkman & Moskowitz 2000, p. 647). We would also add that researchers have seemingly forgone the opportunity to investigate what we actually mean by 'effective coping', and the possibility to explore in detail coping in action; the relationships between coping strategies and what role they play in that relationship (Dewe 2003). Nevertheless, from their powerful and detailed review Folkman and Moskowitz conclude, 'in light of the evidence suggesting that positive affect has significant adaptational functions in the coping process, it becomes important to understand how positive affect is generated and sustained in the context of chronic stress' (2000, p. 650). Their rationale: 'Broadening models of stress and coping to include positive as well as negative affect will change the kinds of questions psychologists ask about coping' (2000, p. 652).

The growing literature on stress related growth also offers work stress researchers the opportunity to 'change the kinds of questions psychologists ask about coping' (Folkman & Moskowitz 2000, p. 652), particularly when Park (2004, p. 69) sets a research context that offers the opportunity to contribute to what is meant about the nature of growth and 'how growth is achieved' in 'terms of individual adjustment' (*see also* Dewe & Cooper 2017, p. 148). Researchers are advised to 'do more descriptive work in this area' (Park 2004, p. 70). Another avenue for work stress research is in the growing interest in emotion approach coping signalling a shift from the traditional emotion avoidance coping (Austenfield & Stanton 2004; *see* Dewe & Cooper 2017, p. 159). Following the work of Austenfield and Stanton these authors describe emotion approach coping as involving emotion processing (e.g. I take time to figure out what I am really feeling) and emotion expressing (e.g. I feel free to express my emotions) (2004, pp. 1342–1343; *see* Dewe & Cooper 2017, p. 159).

Then adding to these new avenues for research we have more work to do in terms of what we mean by coping effectively and coping flexibility (Cheng 2001; Kato 2012; *see* Dewe & Cooper 2017, pp. 159–162) which also requires more descriptive work. Advancing these issues requires researchers to consider the role of appraisals, also requiring descriptive work, to capture the meanings they give to a stressful encounter, giving a context that is saturated with explanatory potential that enables synthesis to occur in our work (*see* Lazarus 2000, p. 668). Understanding coping flexibility also requires descriptive work since we need to develop our understanding of coping in action, since coping strategies are not 'independent of one another' and 'seem to travel together' (Folkman & Moskowitz 2004, p. 753). This means we need to understand the relationships between coping strategies, the role strategies play in that relationship and how we would describe that relationship. Advancing our understanding of coping effectiveness and coping flexibility are simply grounded in building our knowledge of appraisals and coping in action.

Directions for future research

Coping research 'evolves with the accumulation of research' (Folkman 2011, p. 461). Coping research is, as Lazarus suggests, 'maturing' in the sense that its research will be of 'higher quality' and 'more creative' (Lazarus 2000, p. 673). It is our view as well that creativity and quality should be the hallmark of future coping research as it has already been displayed in the research cited in this chapter. Marking the 'positive assessment' given by Lazarus (2000,

p. 673). Following this tradition this involves not just recognizing the 'complexities inherent in the study of coping' but capturing what Folkman and Moskowitz describe as its 'great promise' (2004, p. 768) by recognizing the changing realities of the workplace and our moral responsibility to those whose working lives we study and their well-being. We outline a number of avenues that lay the foundations for how this may be achieved.

a   We begin these avenues by emphasizing that work stress research needs to acknowledge the significance and explanatory potential that resides in the concept of 'appraisal', and through more descriptive work capturing the meaning that those engaged in a stressful encounter give it. This sets the crucial context that gives the stressful transaction its meaning and is something that has been lost to work stress research. This also gives us the context to explore coping in action, investigating the relationship between coping strategies, describing the nature of that relationship and giving meaning to the expression that coping strategies 'seem to travel together' (Folkman & Moskowitz 2004, p. 753). This approach is crucial to better understand the interdependence of coping strategies and the grounding for understanding coping in action.

b   We should now begin to explore how cyberbehaviours can be integrated into coping research, so that our research captures the changing nature of the realities of work. The idea that surrounds the dualism of technology should motivate researchers to discover the role that cyber behaviours have in advancing our knowledge of categories of coping strategies.

c   Coupled with (b), we should recognize the importance of refining measures and make them reflective of the realities of work. This means we should explore how cyberbehaviours change the nature of stressors and other constructs, marking the significance of refining as a tool whose time has come in how we conduct our research.

d   We should also be ready to explore how cyberbehaviours redefine behaviours like 'busyness' and 'productivity', and in this context explore what this means for stress research. One direction could be by returning to those autogenic coping techniques and considering their role in giving, in a 24/7 digital everywhereness world, that sense of mindfulness and the importance that solitude (Newport 2019) has in such a world. Again, reflecting on what this means for coping research.

e   Returning to the positive psychology movement and focus on the role of positive affect in coping research. Indeed, looking more specifically at the role of 'discrete emotions' in our research, giving presence to the crucial role of appraisal and giving a context and synthesis to our work reflecting the transactional nature of the stressful encounter.

Chapter 5

The future of work stress research

The changing nature of our discipline

We believe work stress research has reached a tipping point. Why? Because 'recent technological advances and their associated consequences have altered the fundamental chemistry of work' (Muchinsky 2006, p. 3). Organizations are in 'perpetual motion' (Baruch & Hind 1999, p. 295). These changes are a powerful reminder for researchers to not just ask where our theories are taking us, but how well they express the realities of working lives. We must also ask what does it mean to be an applied discipline, and how can we give voice to the 'empathy for much of what workers in fact experience on the job' (Lefkowitz 2011, p. 113). Our argument is not with our 'technical competence', but that we are also a 'values driven' discipline, which creates a moral responsibility we have to those whose working lives we study. The turbulence of the changes that are turning working lives on their head now makes this responsibility crucial. This requires us to acknowledge that we are at a tipping point and the best way to give our discipline the identity we espouse is to return our focus back to our 'humanist' roots (*see* Lefkowitz 2008, p. 444). Progress can only be achieved if we return to the 'values' side of the equation, and in such a dynamically changing world, focus our attention in a way that ensures our work captures the realities of contemporary working life and their consequences for individual health and well-being.

How do we confront this tipping point? We do it through raising the importance of the concept of relevance, because of its potential potency, power and significance at this time. Particularly thinking in terms of a view of relevance that emphasizes its 'moral responsibility' dimension, and through this focus the meaning it gives to individual well-being. Relevance is 'a long-standing theme', but there is little evidence that we have paid 'serious attention to' it (Corley & Gioia 2011, p. 21). Perhaps, it is, that we have simply given attention to it primarily when it is directed towards its role in supporting our 'technical competence' (Lefkowitz 2011, p. 114). In this way, the moral and social values of relevancy have been overshadowed. However, relevance unleashes the forces which give other elements like refinement, meaning and context their legitimacy, authority, and power. We have turned to these concepts before (Dewe & Cooper 2012; 2017). As a collective, these elements give our work a platform and scope which goes beyond our 'technical competence', although not denying its importance. They give meaning and balance to our research. These elements stand as a test of the relevance of our research, and its ability to capture the realities of contemporary working and its consequences for well-being.

Our argument follows the work of Lefkowitz (2008; 2011) where he explains how the science (S)-practitioner (P) model should be expanded, and 'replaced' to explicitly include the humanist (H) dimension, as this points to the 'heritage of psychology' and part of our moral responsibilities not forgetting our 'professional obligations'. (2008, p. 442). In this way, our work is 'marked' not just by our technical competence but also by its humanist concerns (*see* Muchinsky 2006, p. 11). As Lefkowitz (2008) explains, while we question the robustness of our technical competence, we should also acknowledge our moral responsibilities to capture a broader view of our work and our profession. The time is right to take this stance, particularly in a world that is as challenging as it is turbulent to point to our 'humanist' concerns to better understanding the realities of working lives and the consequences this has for individual well-being. It seems to us that acknowledging the role of relevancy, and through it the tools of refinement, meaning and context work stress research, is well suited to take these ideas forward. In the research cited in this book we have witnessed that many researchers appeared to have already accepted this call. We are simply building on this volume of work and fulfilling our moral responsibilities to those whose working lives we study.

What does this mean for organizational psychology?

We can understand what this means for organizational psychology by pointing to four themes emerging from our research that reflect the tipping points that challenge us to articulate the realities of contemporary working lives. These four themes are: the distinction between work and jobs, the integration of cyberpsychology, the explanatory potential of meaning/context and the nature of well-being. Explaining these themes will set the context and provide a platform that allows us, later in this chapter, to give in more detail possible potential future directions for work stress research.

Work as distinct from jobs

One of the themes cited throughout this book is the need to acknowledge that the future requires that we think more in terms of 'work' as distinct from 'jobs', since 'work [is becoming] a tradable commodity rather than a job' (Maitland & Thomson 2011, p. 149). This distinction is well expressed by a number of authors as it gives a better understanding of the realities of contemporary working lives (Donkin 2010; Gratton 2014; Kessler 2019; Maitland & Thomson 2011; Mulcahy 2017). Others point to the dramatically changing nature of employment arrangements, which also express the realities of contemporary working life (Ashford *et al.*, 2007; Marler *et al.*, 2002; Smith 2002; Spreitzer *et al.*, 2017).

Why is this distinction important? Because it foreshadows 'what the future [of work] might look like' (Kessler 2019, p. 250). As Spreitzer and colleagues make clear, this distinction is needed simply because it captures the realities of contemporary working that is now 'firmly rooted in the new world of work' and 'here to stay' (2017, p. 475). To support this distinction, many focus on flexibility when describing the key characteristic of this new work, 'flexibility in the employment relationship, flexibility in the scheduling of work and flexibility in where work is accomplished' (Spreitzer *et al.*, 2017, p. 473). The focus on flexibility when describing this work offers an avenue for future researchers to explore. How should flexibility be defined, and what it means in reality, how is it managed, and by whom, and how it shapes the working experience and the dynamics of working (*see* Spreitzer *et al.*, 2017). This way of working has already prompted commentators to argue, when employment is being categorized, then a new category is now needed to express this contemporary way of working (Kessler 2019). But shadowing this distinction is a second theme that signals the direction research should take: exploring how people actually experience this work in this new economy (*see* Petriglieri *et al.*, 2018).

This distinction is fundamental. Why? Simply because this type of work is growing exponentially in many different forms, and so we must direct future research towards looking for ways 'which can help us understand the everyday experiences of these workers' (Spreitzer *et al.*, 2017, p. 486). Couple this with calls for a more 'nuanced' approaches since 'we need to recognize the range of experience in [this type of] work' (Rogers 2000, p. 2), and how 'care must be taken to tailor the ideas to the specific ways' this type of work is different (Ashford *et al.*, 2007, p. 80). Not forgetting a 'continuing need for more detailed, fine-grained studies' (Cappelli & Keller 2013, p. 898). Smith (2002, p. 4) also argues that it is best to 'look at these changes and arrangements [in work] through the eyes of the workers participating in them'. These comments suggest that 'a good starting point may be qualitative work' (Spreitzer *et al.*, 2017, p. 486).

Add to this that the term work is 'socially constructed', and the need to understand the experiences of contemporary working helps us understand how 'over time norms about employment change' (Ashford *et al.*, 2007, p. 74). This means that we need to follow the mantra of Ashford and colleagues to release 'our imagination about organization behavior' and 'examine needs to expand [it] accordingly' bringing research on the realities of contemporary work on to 'central stage' (2017, pp. 106; 98) where it now belongs; meaning that a focus on how workers actually experience the realities of these working arrangements is essential. This focus should be the next direction organizational psychology research takes when attempting to understand the very core of this way of working.

Refining the concept of employability

The focus on work, and the realities of the experience of contemporary work, spills over and points to a need to refine other concepts in the wake of these working life changes. These include employability, job security, managing this work and job crafting. We explore these concepts in the context of future research. Turning first to employability, we highlight it in terms of two themes: (a) it's meaning as a style of working and (b) what is needed to sustain this style of working. Thinking of 'employability' as reflecting a style of working, we need to ensure that this theme captures the idea that the nature of employment is transitioning 'from being defined by job, organization and place in the hierarchy, it will increasingly be about a person's skills, reputation and ability to contribute and build networks' (Maitland & Thomson 2011, p. 153). As a term that reflects a style of working, employability has always reflected a sensitivity to change. Its history and roots locate it in the uncertainty and insecurity of work. These elements are well known as attributes that reflect the realities of 21st century working, simply because work is 'intertwined with temporariness and risk' (Smith 2002, p. 7). This sensitivity to change, and its history, should mean employability should now be refined to focus on work 'rather than the pursuit of jobs' (Smith 2002, p. 178).

When it comes to the second theme of what is needed to sustain this style of working, it seems that employability researchers have produced a growing volume of research (*see* Dewe & Cooper 2017, pp. 117–119) that focuses on 'individual self-development', where the emphasis is on growing one's ability for being continuously employed (Forrier & Sels 2003), or refining one's capability to 'make employment transitions' (De Cuyper, Bernhard-Oettel, Berntson, De Witte & Alarco 2008, p. 490) or maintaining one's 'attractiveness' to employers (Rothwell & Arnold 2007, p. 24). There is a sense this includes focusing on building the opportunities to broaden your experiences (Petriglieri *et al.*, 2018) or engaging in lifelong learning or what Selingo and Simon (2017, p. 4/5) describe as 'renewable learning'. Researchers may wish to build into their work in the future more directed questions, when exploring how workers actually experience the realities of these contemporary working arrangements and ask about how these workers sustain this way of working. Particularly when exploring the risks associated with this way of working (i.e. intrinsic job security), and its accompanying existential anxieties (*see* Petriglieri *et al.*, 2018). Employability is a concept in transition. If it is to become 'the upcoming critical resource for workers in times of high job insecurity' (De Cuyper & De Witte, 2010, p. 636), it now needs to be refined. So, it captures the realities of contemporary working. In this way it can match these aspirations regarding its place in this 'new era' to 'become the new human resource language' for not just assessing the experience of contemporary working lives, but how they are sustained (Dewe & Cooper 2017, p. 118).

Refining job security and other consequences

Job security also takes on a new meaning when placed in the context of contemporary working arrangements. Researchers believe these arrangements 'represents a different conception of job security' as it now 'is rooted in [the workers] own skills and ability to sell those skills' to employers (Ashford *et al.*, 2007; Marler *et al.*, 2002, p. 430). Ashford and colleagues adding 'supposedly increas[ing] their security through skill accumulation' (Ashford *et al.*, 2007, p. 86). Interestingly, Marler and colleagues, cite research that suggests being able to work across boundaries may lead organizations to view this knowledge as 'new knowledge and this carries great value to an [employing] organization' (2002, p. 430), suggesting that this may also be a potential lever to offer improved security. Marler and colleagues (2002, p. 430), do make it clear that 'skill development is clearly an important component' of contemporary working life. So does Spreitzer and her colleagues when they comment 'the most important strategy for individuals is to have and maintain skills that are in demand', adding that 'individuals must be proactive in learning those skills that are in high demand' (2017, p. 491). This context and these comments give an understanding to why the term 'flexicurity' has entered our vocabulary. Where flexibility and security are 'promoted and combined in some form or another [that] offers new opportunities to establish different approaches to employment policies' (Dewe & Cooper 2017, p. 119; Spreitzer *et al.*, 2017).

But this style of working remains, as Ashford and colleagues makes clear, we 'in general [know] little' about these workers and their working experiences but emphasize that by acknowledging this way of working 'might' offer a way to draw attention to understanding more about the experience of this style of working (Ashford *et al.*, 2007, p. 86). While Kessler (2019, p. 248), notes that we must, if this style of working is to be sustained, ensure that the 'support systems' are 'in place' and 'prepared to handle the major changes on the horizon' going on to reflect that without these support systems 'it can't quite count as progress'. Offering another pathway for future research.

These issues also give a sense of new meaning to 'job crafting'. As it widens its nature and scope giving workers the flexibilities 'to craft [work] and life that meet[s] their own needs' and how these workers 'can also craft their own sense of purposeful work' (Spreitzer *et al.*, 2017, pp. 493; 491). It also challenges and gives new meaning to how these workers are managed either in their work roles or personally (Ashford *et al.*, 2007). This requires new management styles (Ashford *et al.*, 2007). We need new leadership approaches and new human resource procedures (Marler *et al.*, 2002) to manage these workers, as much as they likewise learn to manage themselves as they are free of all the attributes that follow a job or a traditional career. Presenting a further path for future research. In this way 'self-control or self-management is thus a defining feature of new work systems' (Gephart 2002, p. 335).

All these concepts, future working, employability, job security, job crafting and management are intimately intertwined. This simply means that we should now begin to focus our research on better understanding how these contemporary working arrangements are experienced and sustained. It is these insights that will become crucial in directing our research towards new meanings and new pathways that gives our work relevance. It is uncovering and understanding these nuances about contemporary working life that will meet the moral and professional responsibilities of our discipline, and it is surely these responsibilities that have inspired those whose work we have cited. It is these changes that 'underscore the importance of "new work" studies' (Gephart 2002, p. 343). It is this work that will give us the pathways and the knowledge to offer all workers the opportunity to flourish in these contemporary working arrangements. Recognizing that it is a choice they make rather than they 'default to it' simply because their options are limited (Spreitzer *et al.*, 2017, p. 485).

The integration of cyberpsychology into our work

The arrival of cyber psychology offers us a time to reflect on the world we live in, that includes at the bare minimum both a 'digital everywhereness' (Scott 2016, p. 17) and 'digital distraction[s]' (Watson 2018, p. 15) that are impossible to ignore because they drive 'our hyper-complex habitat' (Shadbolt & Hampson 2018, p. 26). Leaving commentators to question whether this lifestyle is sustainable (Newport 2019, p. x), and is it the sort of world we want (Turkle 2012). It is now time to integrate this world into work stress research. This means future research should begin at this broad contextual level, before turning its focus towards the role cyberbehaviours play specifically in the world of work.

Why begin with this broad contextual focus? Why shouldn't we just begin by focusing on, and prioritizing, the specific ways cyberpsychology can be integrated into work stress research? It is our view that starting our research in this way gives us a broader canvass which we can work too, and against which we can assess our findings. This 'hyper-complex habitat' (Shadbolt & Hampson 2018) has simply seeped into all aspects of life and living, deftly and cleverly crossing boundaries, and raising questions about the life it is crafting for us. It's speed of effect has made it almost impossible to ignore, and its meaning now holds significant explanatory potential. Measuring this 'hyper-complex habitat' offers a platform for contextualizing the more specific work findings when research turns to that focus. So, the first step in researching the integration of cyberpsychology into work stress research is to explore the 'type of measures' we need that capture this hyper-complex habitat to provide the broader canvass that will enable us to better understand the way that cyberbehaviours are shaping work and its dynamics. Remembering that it was Lazarus (2000, p. 668) who laid down that 'detailed description' is an important part to our science.

Work researchers have already begun to explore the idea of 'redesigning work for a digital workforce' and the 'mindful usage of technology' (Colbert et al., 2016, p. 735). We begin with the 'mindful use of technology' as this gives us the context to explore the role cyberbehaviours may play in broadening our views of coping. This is not the only future direction for research that involves cyberbehaviours as we also point to how cyberbehaviours have changed the way we understand 'busyness' and 'being productive'. So, another avenue for future research would be to explore how cyberbehaviours have begun to change the common language of management. Exploring changing behaviours also means that future research needs to investigate the nature of the synergetic relationship between people and machines. The management literature suggests that this relationship is best built on collaboration (Lake 2019, p. 28) with support from scholars who suggest the future is built on collaboration rather than competition (Harari 2018). The next step is to develop our understanding of what we mean by collaborating with, and partnering with a machine, not forgetting how collaborating and partnering are managed, and what skills managers need to effectively navigate such relationships.

The research (Lim & Chen 2012) that gives us 'cyberloafing', turned to the language of coping when explaining its findings. In this way it captured the 'digital fluency' of the workforce, and offers the opportunity to explore if cyberloafing marks its place as a coping strategy and an example of the 'mindful use of technology' (Colbert et al., 2016, pp. 732; 735). It is our belief that it is now time to integrate the reality of working lives into coping research by building on the work of cyberloafing. This approach would simply follow the traditions of coping research where the classifying of coping strategies builds on our evolving knowledge, meaning that we now need to acknowledge the role of technology and its associated behaviours in coping research.

Technology via cyberbehaviours has begun to change the common language of management and, indeed organizational psychology. Future research needs to acknowledge how meanings are changing and determine the consequences for leadership styles and human resource management procedures. One example of changing meanings surrounds what we now understand by being busy and productive actually means (*see* Newport 2016; Watson 2018). This illustrates how cyber behaviours are shaping how we work leaving future researchers to now explore what this actually means for the dynamics of management interactions. Similarly, when thinking about the synergetic relationship between people and machines, future research needs to explore what we mean when we ask 'what is a relationship' (Turkle 2012, p. 19), or what the answer is to the question 'are you good at working with intelligent machines or not?' (Cowen 2014, p. 4). Likewise, what do we mean by collaborating and partnering with a machine? Exploring the work of Wilson and Daugherty (2019, p. 143), who gave us what they describe as 'fusion skills', may give us a clue as to how to frame this research. These examples illustrate the need for a broad canvass of research simply because the impact and influence of technology, and its associated behaviours, is far reaching, varied and complex. It also points to the need to place 'detailed description' (Lazarus 2000, p. 668) as a prescribed strategy at the heart of this research. All giving urgency to Kessler's call that what we have ahead of us when thinking of the future of work and its meaning is 'the slow, hard work that we must do to prepare for it' (2019, p. 250).

The explanatory potential of meaning and context

We have argued throughout this book that the significance of relevance should be elevated and given a higher status in the minds of researchers, because it heralds the key to assessing our work, the value of our contributions, and what it is that we accomplish (*see* Muchinsky 2006). Coupled with this we have argued that relevance includes a powerful moral responsibility to those whose working lives we study. It is this component of relevance that drives our work to focus on our humanist traditions of concern for individual well-being. Relevance also emphasizes that our accomplishments have only value if our work capture the realities of working lives and their consequences for well-being. This view of relevance also gives strength and power to other tools that that ensure our research is directed at the realities of work giving authority to our discipline. It is establishing meanings that are relevant which intimately generates the power and explanatory potential that resides in understanding the contexts our work is embedded in. Much of this chapter has turned to the refining of meanings so they match the realities of contemporary working. From this comes the fashioning of the context in which our research is embedded.

It is Folkman that describes the stress model as 'contextual' (2009, p. 74), making the need to acknowledge just how crucial context is to our understanding of the stress process. As we have in the past (Dewe & Cooper 2012; 2017), we turn again to the concept of primary appraisal – the meanings given to stressful encounters to emphasize its fundamental role in work stress generally. It is a personal context that informs 'the quality of the individual's emotional response' and 'to the ways in which the person cope[s]' (Folkman & Moskowitz 2004, p. 746). Lazarus (1993, pp. 243–244) describes it in this way, 'I am confident that personal meanings are the most important aspects of psychological stress with which the person must cope.' This is probably the most powerful context that stress researchers will encounter. It represents a fundamental element in our synthesis of the stress process that still alludes work stress researchers. It provides the 'detailed description' (Lazarus 2000, p. 668) that is becoming more significance to stress research, and organizational psychology more generally, provoking researchers to acknowledge its role, its importance and its powerful explanatory potential. Future research should turn to this context of personal meaning and restore it to its rightful place in stress research. Porter (Porter 2008, p. 525) gives us a clear signal about the importance of context suggesting that we should give it along with change 'more concentrated research'.

The nature of well-being

We believe that the surfacing of four themes in organizational psychology gives a sense of the direction future research, should take if it is to meet the challenges of the tipping point it faces. Each theme, in its own way, focuses on re-uniting well-being with its humanistic roots proposing that our concentration is directly centred on the individual at work (*see* Lefkowitz 2008; 2011). The first theme captures this need 'for our concern to be [directed] for the well-being of the individual worker' focusing on 'what [that] experience of work ought to be' (Lefkowitz 2011, pp. 114; 113). This theme and the three that follow simply reflect the importance of relevance. Particularly its dimension that points us to our responsibilities to those whose working lives we research. The second theme reflects the growing interest in human capital (Lefkowitz 2008; 2011). This interest, and the different perspectives that now describe this type of capital, offers 'a new discourse, a greater awareness and a need, perhaps more compelling than before, to better represent those invisible resources ... that capture the "dynamics of value creation" in organizations' (Dewe & Cooper 2017, p. 190; Fincham & Roslender 2003, p. 782). These perspectives on human capital, build a context within which employees 'can flourish' and develop (Roslender 2009, p. 343). The third theme follows the developing interest in human capital and explores the ideas of happiness and what makes good work (Coats & Lekhi 2008), arguing that work needs to be 'a fully human activity' emphasizing job quality and 'a life that they value' (Coats & Lekhi 2008, p. 13). The final theme explores the role of technology in shaping work and raises the question of 'what else might we do to make work more people-centric in an age of machines?' arguing that 'the real value of work' lies in 'what it produces in us' and in an age of rampant digital everywhereness asks are we forgetting 'what it means to be human' (Watson 2018, pp. 181; 187; 240). So, to meet the moral responsibilities that we have to those whose working lives we study, and the responsibilities we have as a profession, we should, if we are to challenge the tipping point we face, focus our attention and place it directly on a concern for the well-being of the individual at work (see Lefkowitz 2008; 2011).

A more detailed focus on future directions for work stress research

The tipping point we face challenges us to articulate the realities of contemporary working and its consequences for well-being. Doing so provides us, argues Ashford and her colleagues (2007, p. 67), with a context 'for testing and developing theory about organizations, work, and workers' adding 'the time is ripe' for exploring new theories and expanding and refining existing theories (Ashford *et al.*, 2007, p. 79), reinforcing 'the value we bring' as a discipline since its value is measured by 'what we [can] accomplish' (Muchinsky 2006, p. 9). Building on the platform of research we have discussed above and the context it creates, we set out more details about the future directions work stress research may take.

Technology and future directions of work stress research

It is time to take our research when considering technology and the way it is shaping working lives and behaviours, and life generally, and place it onto a broader canvass, acknowledging on the way the good work that has already focused on techno stress (Ragu-Nathan, Tarafdar & Ragu-Nathan 2008; Tarafdar, Cooper & Stich 2019). It is this broader canvass that draws attention to wider issues that need to be framed into our research. For example, we need to think 'about who we are and where we are going and the need for human beings to remain central to any new digital interests or perspectives' (Watson 2018, p. xv). We need to explore the type of leadership needed in this digital age. Here we may wish to take the work by Schwab (2018b), and frame research around 'systems leadership'. Directing research that captures the nature of 'systems leadership', that allows us to focus on its ability to 'cultivate a shared vision for change' and how it creates 'a renaissance that is human-centred' (Schwab 2018b, p. 228), not forgetting how it enables us 'to think more deeply about the relationship between technology, and society, understanding the ways in which our collective actions (and inactions) create the future' (Schwab 2018b, p. 220). This focus also resonates with the demands for a more humanist direction to well-being as it complements, directs attention and attends to the impact of technology on us and society, providing an opportunity to think about how we, can direct our research so that it 'influenc[es] and guid[es] how systems that surround us and shape our lives' (Schwab 2018b, p. 8).

The management literature also points to research opportunities, since managers are already making choices in organizations about technology. We should recognize this as a time to engage with this research. Exploring what the elements of good practice may be when organizations approach the introduction of technological innovations. This research would offer managers a context when introducing technology to consider issues surrounding developing trust in technology, issues surrounding collaboration, partnering, and understanding technologies risks and limitations, not forgetting how this is managed and what new skills will be required to manage in such an environment. Continuing this theme of a broader canvas, we may wish to explore the new meanings we give to 'being present' in a digital age and what it means to be 'here and there' (Scott 2016, p. 15).

As discussed earlier in this chapter, we need to develop a measure that captures the meaning of our 'digital everywhereness' (Scott 2016, p. 6) which provides a context to understand the ease with which technology crosses boundaries between the virtual world and reality and into working life, and what this means for the quality of working life. We have acknowledged the need to integrate cyber behaviours, focusing on cyberloafing into coping research and how that research simply follows the tradition of using our evolving knowledge of coping to redefine the classification of coping strategies, so that any schema of coping strategies captures the realities of contemporary working lives. While we should not underestimate the power, authority and benefits that accompanies technological innovation, nor should we underestimate in our research issues like ethics, privacy, security, and the ownership of, and the sharing of data (Lanier 2014). All of which questions technology's limits and boundaries, and its sustainability. We should also question just how this level, and rate of innovation is sustainable simply because of the ways it shapes our lives, our behaviours and the unquestioning priority we give it to do such things.

Work and the future directions of work stress research

Earlier in this chapter we signalled the need to acknowledge that the future requires that we think more in terms of work as distinct from jobs. We pointed to a growing and crucial literature that explores the idea that work will become the important currency not jobs. As this distinction, simply points to 'what the future [of work] might look like' (Kessler 2019, p. 250), and how this distinction is now 'firmly in the new world of work' and 'here to stay' (Spreitzer *et al.*, 2017, p. 475). The consequences of these changes mean that individuals will rely more heavily on marketing their 'unique skills, reputation and "personal brand"' (Maitland & Thomson 2011, p. 152), and as Mulcahy (2017, p. 6) succinctly points to 'where once were *jobs*, there is increasingly just *work*'.

This has far reaching implications for our theories, our models, our discipline, and our measures as the context and reality of working lives is significantly changed. The urgency and significance of this change and its consequences is reflected in Mulcahy (2017, p. 189) comments, 'stick[ing] stubbornly to an old outdated model that defines "jobs" and "employees" in ways that are increasingly irrelevant and obstruct innovation, growth, and opportunity'. However, this body of literature also offers two directions future research should take. The first now directs research towards exploring how people actually experience this type of working in this new economy (Petriglieri *et al.*, 2018). The second directs research towards what is needed for workers to actually sustain this style of working.

We agree with the comments by Spreitzer and her colleagues when they suggest that 'a good starting point may be qualitative work' (2017, p. 486). This would provide the crucial 'detailed description' that Lazarus (2000, p. 668) suggests is becoming more significant to our work. Taking this approach to understand how this type of work is experienced, and how it is sustained provides the opportunity to develop a structure around this experience. Giving not just the meanings that exemplify this experience but an explanatory context that offers a deeper, more meaningful understanding of the experience. This sits neatly with the calls reflected in the literature, for more 'nuanced' approaches to understand the 'everyday experiences of these workers' (Spreitzer *et al.*, 2017, p. 486). Researchers will, of course, decide the best way forward. However, capturing the nature of this experience represents to us, the foundation knowledge our work needs to maintain its relevance, and our obligation to those whose working lives we study, as it simply reflects the reality of contemporary working. This is the first crucial step that must be taken as it reflects 'what the future might look like, and the slow, hard work that we must do to prepare for it' (Kessler 2019, p. 250). This is why we must make it our primary focus.

Earlier in this chapter we discussed the consequences of this work versus job distinction, on concepts like employability, job security leading to flexicurity, job crafting, and management and how research should focus on refining their meaning as it is these changes that 'underscore the importance of "new work" studies' (Gephart 2002, p. 343). In this context of changing meanings, researchers need to acknowledge that more work will be necessary when we consider careers, as these changes will 'have enormous implications about how we think about managing our careers and structuring our lives' (Mulcahy 2017, p. 3) since 'people will have more careers during their working lives' (Maitland & Thomson 2011, p. 152).

Accompanying this work on careers, there will be a need to explore 'what support systems' are 'in place' (Kessler 2019, p. 248) to support this new type of working. Exploring the skills necessary to sustain this work and particularly, when exploring, the idea that workers will need to be 'proactive in [their] learning', (Spreitzer *et al.*, 2017, p. 491) then, how do they engage in learning? What appears to be the key to the future will be the importance of lifelong learning and 'renewable learning' (Selingo & Simon 2017, p. 4/5). If, as suggested, 'self-control or self-management is thus a defining feature of new work systems' (Gephart 2002, p. 335), then this offers new pathways for research when exploring careers and the skills necessary to sustain contemporary working styles. Flexibility is fundamental in expressing the nature of contemporary working arrangements. Yet there is still work to be done in its meanings across its different perspectives; flexibility in employment relations, in scheduling work, and in where work is accomplished. These are carefully discussed by Spreitzer and her colleagues, where they offer directions this research may take (*see* Spreitzer *et al.*, 2017, p. 487).

There is more to come when the theme of changing meanings is explored. Turning our attention to traditionally measured role stressors (overload, conflict and ambiguity) opens another pathway for research. Here the focus is on the changing nature of these three role stressors. Role overload will need to be refined because concepts like 'busyness' (Newport 2016) and 'productivity' (Watson 2018) have radically been influenced by technology giving new meanings to overload. In the case of conflict there has been dramatic changes in how we communicate and relate to people. Research points to how the world is 'even more technologically and social wired than ever before' (Barjis, Gupta & Sharda 2011, p. 615), and how 'cyber-incivility' can often be perceived in emails (Andersson & Pearson 1999; Hair, Renaud & Ramsey 2007; Reinke & Chamorro-Premuzic 2014) points to ways we may refine the meaning of role conflict. Ambiguity is similarly in need of being refined because 'more ambiguity around professional affiliations and identities' (Spreitzer *et al.*, 2017, p. 491) will give new meanings to the ambiguities that lie in wait in a digital age.

Summary

This chapter could be viewed as having all the hallmarks of a 'to do' list. But it is much more, particularly when you embed it in a context of crisis, where our discipline is at a tipping point, where the world is being described as entering an 'age of bewilderment' (Harari 2018, p. xiii). Not forgetting the digital distractions that are shaping our lives, accompanied by the constant and relentless challenges of techno-innovations 'symbolic of our quest for convenience and [so called] efficiency' (Watson 2018, p. 6). At the core of this constantly swirling turmoil the world of work, is itself being turned upside down. Ominously challenging us, if we wish to understand the changing nature of work, to embrace new pathways that release us from old traditions and calls us to acknowledge that the way forward must, at the very least, involve our moral responsibilities to those whose working lives we study, accepting that now is the time, as never before, to place our humanistic values at the centre of our endeavours.

All is not lost. We have as a discipline now reached a point, where we are better prepared to structurally distinguish contemporary working arrangements and the roles that flexibility plays in these arrangements. But it is the next step that is the crucial one. It is where we build the context surrounding these structural arrangements, by capturing the 'detailed description' (Lazarus 2000, p. 668) that 'help[s] us understand the everyday experiences of these' working arrangements (Spreitzer *et al.*, 2017, p. 486), and what is needed for workers to actually sustain this style of working. This is what Ashford and her colleagues (2007, p. 106) described as 'expand[ing] accordingly' our 'imagination about organizational behaviour, about appropriate constructs, and about important processes' that '[are] central to filling in a portrait of this new future'. This is the pathway that gives our work, and our discipline a sense of relevance, and fulfils our responsibilities to those whose working lives we study. But these steps are simply the beginning of giving new meanings to our work, and our discipline. These steps arguably begin what is a fundamentally crucial and extensive programme of research and exploration, that captures the realities of the dramatic and formidable challenges we face. We owe this not just to our discipline, but to future generations who will be those who become the recipients of these working lives.

We are moving further and further away from the observations of Studs Terkel (1974, p. xi) about the nature of work, in his acclaimed book *Working*, when he concluded, after having interviewed hundreds of workers:

> work is … about violence to the spirit as well as the body. It is about ulcers as well as accidents, about shouting matches as well as fistfights, about nervous breakdowns as well as kicking the dog around. It is above all … about daily humiliations.

Our work in the work stress field can make a difference by creating healthier and job satisfying employment in a dramatically changing workplace. But to ensure we make that difference our responsibilities must now rest on beginning a process of challenging and refining accepted pathways.

References

Acemoglu, D. (2017). *Review: On robotics, AI and the future of Work.* Reviewed by Juanita Bawagan. www.cifar.ca/cifarnews/2017/06/28/review-daron-acemoglu-on-robotics-ai-and-the-future-of-work (p. 1/5–5/5).

Aldwin, C. M. (2000). *Stress, coping and development: An integrative perspective.* New York: The Guilford Press.

Andersson, L. M., & Pearson, C. M. (1999). Tit for tat? The spiralling effect of incivility in the workforce. *Academy of Management Review* 24, 452–471.

Ansell, M. (2016). Jobs for life are a thing of the past. Bring on lifelong learning. *Guardian* 31 May (p. 1–3).

Ardern, J. Rt Hon. (2019). *Opinion: An economics of kindness.* IBeehive.govt.nz. Originally published by the Financial Times: 22 January 2019.

Artz, B., Goodall, A., & Oswald, A. J. (2016). If your boss could do your job, you're more likely to be happy at work. *Harvard Business Review* (digital article) 29 December. hbr.org/2016/12/if-your-boss-could-do-your-job-youre-more-likely-to-be-happy-at-work

Ashford, S. J., George, E., & Blatt, R. (2007). Old assumptions, new work. *The Academy of Management Annuals* 1, 65–117.

Austenfield, J. L., & Stanton, A. L. (2004). Coping through emotional approach: A new look at emotion, coping, and health-related outcomes. *Journal of Personality* 72, 1335–1363.

Barjis, J., Gupta, A., & Sharda, R. (2011). Knowledge work and communication challenges in networked enterprises. *Information Systems Frontiers* 13, 615–619.

Barling, J., & Griffiths, A. (2003). A history of occupational health psychology. In J. C. Quick & L. E. Tetrick (Eds). *Handbook of occupational health psychology* (pp. 19–33). Washington, DC: American Psychological Association.

Barsade, S. G., Brief, A. P., & Spataro, S. E. (2003). The affective revolution in organizational behavior: The emergence of a paradigm. In J. Greenberg (Ed.). *Organizational behavior: The state of the science* (pp. 3–52). Mahwah, NJ: Lawrence Erlbaum Associates.

Baruch, Y. (2005). Bullying on the net: Adverse behavior on e-mail and its impact. *Information & Management* 42, 361–371.

Baruch, Y., & Hind, P. (1999). Perpetual motion in organizations. Effective management and the impact of the new psychological contracts on 'survival syndrome'. *European Journal of Work and Organizational Psychology* 8, 295–306.

Berners-Lee, T. (2019). *Stop web's downward plunge to dysfunctional future.* (12 March) www.bbc.com/news/technology-475244744.

Bevan, S., Brinkley, I., Bajorek, R., & Cooper, C. (2018). *21st century workforces and Workplaces.* London: Bloomsbury Business

Black, C. (2008). *Working for a healthier tomorrow: Review of the health of Britain's working age population.* Presented to the Secretary of State for Health and the Secretary of State for Work and Pensions. London: TSOP, 17 March.

Blumer, H. (1969). *Symbolic Interactionism: Perspective and method.* Englewood Cliffs, NJ: Prentice-Hall.

Braun, V., & Clarke, V. (2006). Using thematic analysis in psychology. *Qualitative Research in Psychology* 3, 77–101.

Brod, C. (1982). Managing technostress. Optimizing the use of computer technology. *Personnel Journal* 61, 753–757.

Brown, A., Charlwood, C., Forde, C., & Spencer, D. (2006). *Changing job quality in Great Britain 1998–2004.* Employment Relations Research Series No 70. London: DTI.

Brynjolfsson, E., & McAfee, A. (2014). *The second machine age: Work, progress, and prosperity in a time of brilliant technologies.* New York: W. W. Norton & Company Inc.

Brynjolfsson, E., & McAfee, A. (2011). *Race against the machine.* Lexington: Digital Frontier Press.

Burke, R. (2002). Work stress and coping in organizations: Progress and prospects. In E. Frydenberg (Ed.). *Beyond coping: Meeting goals, visions and challenges* (pp. 83–106). Oxford: Oxford University Press.

Cameron, K. S., Dutton, J E., & Quinn, R. E. (Eds) (2003). *Positive organizational scholarship: Foundations of a new discipline.* San Francisco: BK Publishers Inc.

Cappelli, P. H., & Keller, J., R. (2013). A study of the extent and potential causes of alternative employment arrangement. *Industrial Labour Relations Review* 66, 876–901.

Cascio, W. F. (2007). The new human equation. *The Industrial-Organizational Psychologist* 44, 15–22.

Cheng, C. (2001). Assessing coping flexibility in real-life and laboratory settings: A multimethod approach. *Journal of Personality and Social Psychology* 80, 814–833.

Chiang, I-P., & Su, Y-H. (2012). Measuring and analysing the causes of problematic internet use. *Cyberpsychology, Behavior and Social Networking* 11, 591–596.

Christensen, C. H., & van Bever, D. C. M. (2014). The capitalist's dilemma. *Harvard Business Review* 92, 60–68.

Chui, M., Manyika, J., & Miremadi, M. (2016). Where machines could replace humans-and where they can't (yet). *McKinsey Quarterly* 3, 58–69. Web.b.ebscohost.com/ehost/delivery?sid=eaae4c4b-a50e-4bfb-831d-e5837d0c10. See also McKinsey Digital www.mckinsey.com/business-functions/digital-mckinsey/our-insights/where-machines-could-replace-humans-and-where-they-cant-yet (1/14–14/14).

Coats, D. (2009). Good work in recessionary times. In D. Coats (Ed.). *Advancing opportunity: The future of work* (pp. 6–12). London: The Smith Institute.

Coats, D., & Lekhi, R. (2008). *'Good work': Job quality in a changing economy.* London: The Work Foundation.

Colbert, A., Yee, N., & George, G. (2016). The digital workforce and the workplace of the future. *Academy of Management Journal* 59, 731–739.

Constable, S., Coats, D., Bevan, S., & Mahdon, M. (2009). *Good jobs.* London: The Work Foundation.

Cooper, C. (2009). The transition from the quality of working life to organizational behavior: The first two decades. *Journal of Organizational Behavior* 30, 3–8.

Corley, K. G., & Gioia, D. A. (2011). Building theory about theory building. What constitutes a theoretical contribution? *Academy of Management Review* 36, 12–32.

Cowen, T. (2014). *Average is over: Powering America beyond the age of the great stagnation.* New York: A Plume Book.

Coyle, D., & Quah, D. (2002). *Getting the measure of the new economy.* London: The Work Foundation.

Coyne, J. C., & Racioppo, M. (2000). Never the twain shall meet? Closing the gap between coping research and clinical intervention research. *American Psychologist* 55, 655–664.

Csikszentmihalyi, M. (1990). *Flow: The psychology of optimal experience.* New York, Harper & Row Publishers.

Davenport, T. H., & Ronanki, R. (2019). Artificial Intelligence for the real world. In HBR's 10 must reads (series). *On AI, analytics, and the new machine age* (pp. 1–17). Boston: Harvard Business Review Press.

De Cuyper, N., & De Witte, H. (2010). Temporary employment and perceived employability: Mediated by impression management. *Journal of Career Development* 37, 635–652.

De Cuyper, N., Bernhard-Oettel, C., Berntson, E., De Witte, H., & Alarco, B. (2008). Employability and employees' well-being. Mediation by job security. *Applied Psychology: An international Review* 57, 488–509.

Dewe, P. (2003). A closer examination of the patterns when coping with work related stress: Implications for measurement. *Journal of Occupational and Organizational Psychology* 76, 517–524.

Dewe, P., & Cooper, C. (2017). *Work stress and coping: Forces of change and challenges.* London: SAGE Publications Ltd.

Dewe, P., & Cooper, C. (2012). *Well-being and work: Towards a balanced agenda*. Basingstoke: Palgrave Macmillan.

Dominion Post (2018). *Wallace and Gromit inspire smart pants* 13 September, (p. 20).

Dominion Post (2019). *Inside job – micro-robots can crawl through blood vessels* 9 March, (p. B3).

Donkin, R. (2010). *The future of work*. Basingstoke: Palgrave Macmillan.

Eggers, D. (2018). Finding a way from under Facebook's thumb. *The Dominion Post*, 17 December, (p. 28–29).

Fincham, R., & Roslender, R. (2003). Intellectual capital accounting as management fashion. A review and critique. *European Accounting Review* 12, 781–795.

Fineman, S. (2004). Getting the measure of emotions – and the cautionary tale of emotional intelligence. *Human Relations* 57, 719–740.

Flanagan, F. (2017). Symposium on work in the 'gig' economy: Introduction. *The Economic and Labour Relations Review* 28, 378–381.

Flaws, B., & Pullar-Strecker, T. (2019). Life insurer offers rewards. *Dominion Post* 22 April (p. 22).

Folkman, S. (2011). Stress, health, and coping synthesis, commentary and future directions. In S. Folkman (Ed.). *The Oxford handbook of stress, health and coping* (pp. 453–462). Oxford: Oxford University Press.

Folkman, S. (2011a). Stress, health, and coping. An overview. In S. Folkman (Ed.). *The Oxford handbook of stress, health and coping* (pp. 3–11). Oxford: Oxford University Press.

Folkman, S. (2009). Questions, answers, issues and next steps in stress and coping research. *European Psychologist* 14, 72–77.

Folkman, S., & Moskowitz, J. T. (2004). Coping: Pitfalls and progress. *Annual Review of Psychology* 55, 745–774.

Folkman, S., & Moskowitz, J. T. (2000). Positive affect and the other side of coping. *American Psychologist* 55, 647–654.

Forrier, A., & Sels, L. (2003). The concept of employability: A complex mosaic. *International Journal of Human Resources Development and Management* 3, 102–124.

Frey, C. B., & Osborne, M. A. (2013). *The future of employment: How susceptible are jobs to computerization*. Oxford: Martin School, University of Oxford.

Frick, W. (2019). When your boss wears metal pants. In HBR's 10 must reads (series): *On AI, Analytics, and the new machine age* (pp. 145–153). Boston: Harvard Business Review Press.

Fritz, A. (2019). *What's behind the confidence of the incompetent? This suddenly popular psychological phenomenon*, www.stuff.co.nz/life-style/109781011/whats-behind-the-confidence-of-the-incompetent-this-suddenly-popular-psychological-phenomenon (1/35–5/35).

Fugate, M., & Kinicki, A. J. (2008). A dispositional approach to employability: Development of a measure and test of implications for employee reactions to organizational change. *Journal of Occupational and Organizational Psychology* 81, 503–527.

Fullerton, T. (2019). Microsoft's moral values. *The Australian* 1 April (p. 23).

Gephart, R. P. (2002). Brave new workplace: Organizational behavior in the electronic age. *Journal of Organizational Behavior* 23, 327–344.

Gratton, L. (2014). *The shift: The future of work is already here.* London: William Collins.

Griffiths, M. D. (1995). Technological addictions. *Clinical Psychology Forum* 76, 14–19.

Griffiths, M. (2010). Internet abuse and internet addiction. *The Journal of Workplace Learning* 22, 463–472.

Guest, D. (2004). The psychology of the employment relationship: An analysis based on the psychological contract. *Applied Psychology: An International Review* 53, 541–555.

Guest, D. (2004a). Flexible employment contracts, the psychological contract and employee outcomes: an analysis and review of the evidence. *International Journal of Management Reviews* 5/6, 1–19.

Graham, L., & Oswald, A. (2010). Hedonic capital, adaptation and resilience. *Journal of Economic Behavior and Organization* 76, 372–384.

Gulati, R. (2007). Tent poles, tribalism, and boundary spanning: The rigor-relevance debate in management research. *Academy of Management Journal* 50, 775–782.

Hair, M., Renaud, K. V., & Ramsay, J. (2007). The influence of self-esteem and locus of control on perceived email-related stress. *Computers in Human Behavior* 23, 2791–2803.

Harari, Y. N. (2018). *21 lessons for the 21st century.* London: Jonathan Cape.

Hart, K. E., & Sasso, T. (2011). Mapping the contours of contemporary positive psychology. *Canadian Psychology* 52, 82–92.

Healy, J., Nicholson, D., & Pekarek, A. (2017) Should we take the gig economy seriously? *Labour & Industry* 27, 232–248.

Hirsch, D. (2005). *Sustaining working lives: A framework for policy and practice.* York: Joseph Rowntree Foundation.

Johnson, V. (2019). That's it, I'm breaking up with social media. *Dominion Post* 26 April 2019 (p. 16).

Johnson, B. T., & Acabchuk, R. L. (2018). What are the keys to longer, happier life? Answers from five decades of health psychology research. *Social Science & Medicine* 196, 218–226.

Johnson, S., Roberson, I., & Cooper, C. (2018). *Productivity and happiness at work.* London: Palgrave Macmillan.

Kato, T. (2012). Development of the Coping Flexibility Scale: Evidence for the coping flexibility hypothesis. *Journal of Counselling Psychology* 59, 262–273.

Kessler, S. (2019). *Gigged: The gig economy: The end of the job and the future of work.* London: Random House Business Books.

Kivunja, C. (2015). Teaching students to learn and to work well with 21st century skills: Unpacking the career and life skills domain of the new learning paradigm. *International Journal of Higher Education* 4, 1–11.

Kobie, N. (2018). Can wearable tech save nurses' time and patients' lives? *Guardian* 20 December, www.theguardian.com/practical-dreamers/2018/dec/20/can-wearable-tech-save-nurses-time-and-patients-lives (1/4–4/4).

Kruger, J., & Dunning, D. (1999). Unskilled and unaware of it: How difficulties in recognizing one's own incompetence leads to inflated self-assessments. *Journal of Personality and Social Psychology* 77, 1121–1134.

Lake, K. (2019). Stitch fix's CEO on Selling personal style to the mass market, In HBR's 10 must reads (series): *On AI, Analytics, and the new machine age* (pp. 19–28). Boston: Harvard Business Review Press.

Lanier, J. (2014). *Who owns the future?* New York: Penguin Books.

Lazarus, R. S. (1993). Coping theory and research: Past, present and future. *Psychosomatic Medicine* 55, 234–247.

Lazarus, R. S. (2000). Toward better research on stress and coping. *American Psychologist* 55, 665–673.

Lazarus, R. S., & Cohen-Charash, Y. (2001). Discrete emotions in organizational life. In R. Payne & C. Cooper (Eds). *Emotions at work: Theory, research and applications for management* (pp. 45–81). Chichester: John Wiley & Sons.

Lefkowitz, J. (2011). The science, practice, and morality of work psychology. *Industrial and Organizational Psychology* 4, 112–116.

Lefkowitz, J. (2008). To prosper organizational psychology should … expand the values of organizational psychology to match the quality of its ethics. *Journal of Organizational Behavior* 29, 439–453.

Levitin, D. J. (2019). *The organized mind.* New York: Penguin Random House.

Lim, V. K. G. (2002). The IT way of loafing on the job: Cyberloafing, neutralizing and organizational justice. *Journal of Organizational Behavior* 23, 675–694.

Lim, V. K. G., Teo, S. H., & Loo, G. L. (2002). How do I loaf here? Let me count the ways. *Communications of the ACM* 45, 66–70.

Lim, V. K. G., & Chen, D. J. Q. (2012). Cyberloafing at the workplace: Gain or drain on work. *Behaviour & Information Technology* 31, 343–353.

Luca, M., Kleinberg, J., & Mullainathan, S. (2019). Algorithms need managers, too. In HBR's 10 must reads: *On AI, analytics, and the new machine age* (pp. 29–38). Boston: Harvard Business Review Press.

Luthans, F., Youssef, C. M., & Avolio, B. J. (2007). *Psychology capital: Developing the human edge.* Oxford: Oxford University Press.

Macik-Frey, M., Quick, J. C., & Nelson, D. L. (2007). Advances in occupational health: From a stressful beginning to a positive future. *Journal of Management* 33, 809–840.

Maitland, A., & Thomson, P. (2011). *Future work: How businesses can adapt and thrive in the new world of work.* Basingstoke: Palgrave Macmillan.

Marler, J. H., Barringer, M. W., & Milkovich, G. T. (2002). Boundaryless and traditional contingent employees: Worlds apart. *Journal of Organizational Behavior* 23, 425–453.

Muchinsky, P. M. (2006). Enhancing industrial/organizational psychology: A challenging mandate at the dawn of the 21st century. *Japanese Association of Industrial/Organizational Psychology Journal* 20, 1–27.

Mulcahy, D. (2017). *The Gig Economy: The complete guide to getting better work, taking more time off, and financing the life you want!* New York: AMACOM.

Myers, D. G. (2007). Costs and benefits of American corporate capitalism. *Psychological Inquiry* 18, 43–47.

Newport, C. (2016). *Deep work: Rules for focused success in a distracted world.* London: Piatkus: An imprint of Little, Brown Book Group.

Newport, C. (2019). *Digital minimalization: On living better with less technology.* New York: Portfolio/Penguin.

Organization for Economic Cooperation and Development (2012). *Measuring well-being and progress: Better life perspective.* Paris: OECD Statistics Directorate.

Organization for Economic Cooperation and Development (2013). *Measuring well-being and progress: Better life perspective.* Paris: OECD Statistics Directorate.

Overall, S. (2008). *Inwardness: The rise of meaningful work.* London: The Work Foundation.

Park, C. L. (2004). The notion of growth following stressful life experiences: Problems and prospects. *Psychological Inquiry* 15, 69–76.

Parker, L., & Bevan, S. (2011). *Good work and our times.* Report to the Good Work Commission. July. London: The Work Foundation.

Petriglieri, G., Ashford, S., & Wrzesniewski, A. (2018). Thriving in the gig economy. *Harvard Business Review* March–April, 140–143.

Pfeffer, J. (2010). Building sustainable organizations: the human factor. *Academy of Management Perspectives* 24, 34–45.

Porter, L. W. (2008). Organizational Psychology: A look backward, outward, and forward. *Journal of Organizational Behavior* 29, 519–526.

Porter, L. W., & Schneider, B. (2014). What was, what is, and what may be in OP/OB. *Annual Review of Organizational Psychology and Organizational Behavior* 1, 1–21.

Porter, M. E., & Heppelmann J. E. (2019). Why every organization needs an augmented reality strategy. In HBR's 10 must reads (series): *On AI, analytics, and the new machine age* (pp. 53–76). Boston: Harvard Business Review Press.

Puranam, P., Alexy, O., & Reitzig, M. (2014). What's 'new' about new forms of organizing? *Academy of Management Review* 39, 162–180.

Ragu-Nathan, T., Tarafdar, M., & Ragu-Nathan, B. (2008). The consequences of technostress for end users in organizations: Conceptual development and empirical validation. *Information Systems Research* 19, 417–433.

Reinke, K., & Chamorro-Premuzic, T. (2014). When email use gets out of control. Understanding the relationship between personality and email overload and their impact on burnout and work engagement. *Computers in Human Behavior* 36, 502–509.

Rogers, J. K. (2000). Temps: The many faces of the changing workplace. Ithaca: Cornell University Press.

Roslender, R. (2009). The prospects for satisfactorily measuring and reporting intangibles. *Journal of Human Resource Costing & Accounting* 13, 338–359.

Roslender, R. (2009a). So tell me again … why do you want to account for people? *Journal of Human Resource Costing & Accounting* 13, 143–153.

Roslender, R., & Fincham, R. (2001). Thinking critically about intellectual accounting. *Accounting, Auditing & Accountability Journal* 14, 383–398.

Roslender, R., Stevenson, J., & Kahn, H. (2006). Employee wellness as intellectual capital: An accounting perspective. *Journal of Human Resource Costing & Accounting* 10, 48–64.

Rothwell, A., & Arnold, J. (2007). Self-perceived employability: Development and validation of a scale. *Personnel Review* 36, 23–41.

Rousseau, D. M., & Fried, Y. (2001). Location, location, location: Contextualizing organizational research. *Journal of Organizational Behavior* 22, 1–13.

Sabella, R. A., Patchin, J. W., & Hinduja, S. (2013). Cyberbullying myths and realities. *Computers in Human Behavior* 29, 2703–2711.

Salmon, K. (2019). *Jobs, robots & us: Why the future of work in New Zealand is in our hands*. Wellington: Bridget Williams Books.

Schwab, K. (2018a). *The urgency of shaping the Fourth Industrial Revolution.* weforum.org/agenda/2018/01/the-urgency-of-shaping-the-fourth-industrial-revolution/

Schwab, K. (2018b). *Shaping the future of the fourth industrial revolution: A guide to building a better world.* United Kingdom: Portfolio Penguin: Penguin Random House UK

Scoble, R., & Israel, S. (2014). *Age of context: Mobile, sensors, data and the future of privacy*. Lexington: Patrick Brewster Press.

Scott, L. (2016). *The four-dimensional human: Ways of being in the digital world*. London: Penguin Random House UK.

Seligman, M. E. P., & Csikszentmihalyi, M. (2000). Positive psychology: An introduction. *American Psychologist* 55, 5–14.

Selingo, J. J., & Simon, K. (2017). *The future of your career depends on lifelong learning*. Forbes 9th October. See also: www.forbes.com/sites/schoolboard/2017/10/09/the-future-of-your-career-depends-on-lifelong-learning/#1eab447c1bd7 (p. 1/5–5/5).

Shadbolt, N., & Hampson, R. (2018). *The digital ape: How to live (in peace) with smart machines*. London: Scribe Publications.

Simmers, C. A., Anandarajan, M., & D'Ovidio, R. (2008). Investigation of the underlying structure of personal web usage in the workplace. *Academy of Management Annual Meeting Proceedings* 1, 1–6.

Smith, V. (2002). *Crossing the great divide: Worker risk and opportunity in the new economy*. Ithaca, New York: Cornell Paperbacks.

Snyder, C. R. (1999). *Coping: The psychology of what works*. New York: Oxford University Press.

Spreitzer, G. M., Cameron, L., & Garrett, L. (2017). Alternative work arrangements: Two images of the new world of work. *Annual Review of Organizational Psychological and Organizational Behavior* 4, 473–499.

Spreitzer, G. M., Porath, C. L., & Gibson, C. B. (2012). Towards human sustainability: How to enable more thriving at work. *Organizational Dynamics* 41, 155–162.

Stanton, J. M. (2002). Company profile of the frequent internet user. *Communications of the ACH* 45, 55–59.

Staub, S., & Kaynak, R. (2014). Is an unskilled really aware of it? *Social and Behavioral Sciences* 150, 899–907.

Stears, M., & Parker, I. (2012). *Responsible capitalism and behavioural change: Evaluating the Social Business Trust and planning for the future.* London: Institute for Public Policy Research.

Stiglitz, J. (2019). Age of upheaval. *New Zealand Listener* 20–26 July (pp. 12–16).

Stiglitz, J. E., Sen, A., & Fitoussi, J. P. (2009). *Report by the Commission on the measurement of economic performance and social progress.* Paris: OECD.

Syal, R., & Stewart, H. (2018) Workers get new rights in overhaul. But zero-hours contracts remain. www.theguardian.com/law/2018/dec/17/workers-get-new-rights-in-overhaul-but-zero-hours-contracts-remain (1/6–4/6).

Tarafdar, M., Cooper, C., & Stich J-F. (2019). The technostress trifecta-Technostress, eustress, techno distress and design: Theoretical directions and an agenda for research. *Infosystems Journal* 29, 6–42.

Tarafdar, M., Tu, Q., & Ragu-Nathan, T. (2010). Impact of technostress on end-user satisfaction and performance. *Journal of Management Information Systems* 27, 303–334.

Tasker, S-J. (2019). Healthcare in the hands of robots. *The Australian*, (1 April) p. 19.

Taylor, M. (2017). *Good work: Review of modern working practices* RSA: July 2017.

Terkel, S. (1974). *Working: People talk about what they do all day and how they feel about what they do.* New York: New Press.

Torres, N. (2018). Are there good jobs in the gig economy? *Harvard Business Review*, July–August 146–147.

Turkle, S. (2012). *Alone together: Why we expect more from technology and less from each other.* New York: Basic Books.

Vermeulen, F. (2007). 'I shall not remain insignificant': Adding a second loop to matter more. *Academy of Management Journal* 50, 754–761.

Warr, P., & Clapperton, G. (2010). *The joy of work? Jobs, happiness, and you.* Hove: Routledge.

Watson, R. (2018). *Digital vs human: How we'll live, love and think in the future.* London: Scribe Publications.

Williams, C. C. (2007). *Rethinking the future of work: Directions and visions.* Basingstoke: Palgrave Macmillian.

Wilson, H. J., & Daugherty, P. R. (2019). Collaborative intelligence: Humans and AI are joining forces. In HBR's 10 must reads (series): In *On AI, analytics, and the new machine age* (pp. 127–143). Boston: Harvard Business Review Press.

Wong, P. T. P. (2011). Positive psychology 2.0: Towards a balanced interactive model of the good life. *Canadian Psychology* 52, 69–81.

Youssef, C. M., & Luthans, F. (2007). Positive organizational behavior in the workplace: The impact of hope, optimism, and resilience. *Journal of Management* 33, 774–800.

Index

ability 28, 32, 45, 68, 70–1, 78; to absorb and act on' information 29; to contribute and build networks 40; to convert 'data and analytics into images that are overlaid on the real world' 29; to learn and to reinvent ourselves 21, 45; as researchers to achieve a more meaningful integration of findings 1; to understand new technologies 19

Acemoglu, D. 47

age 86, 92; of 'bewilderment' 11, 34, 51, 81; networking 18; new machine 86–7, 89–90, 93; the second machine 11, 34; technological 11, 34

Aldwin, C.M. 13, 55

algorithms 10–11, 22, 27, 29

ambiguities in the digital age 81

'analysis thinking' 62

analytics 10, 22, 29, 86–7, 89–90, 93

anxieties 42–3, 71

appraisals 14, 56, 61–6; cognitive 61; individual's 62; role of 62, 64

approaches 48, 70, 80; appraisal-centered 62; contextual 50; dispositional 87; emotional 84; human-centered 24; incremental 10, 25, 27; multimethod 85

AR *see* augmented reality

artificial intelligence 10, 22, 25–7, 86

artificial muscles 30

attributes 41, 71–2; that reflect the realities of twenty-first century working 71

attributes to operate successfully 41

augmented reality 10, 22, 29

Austenfield, J.L. 64

autogenic techniques 20

automation 28, 48–50; and cars 22; cognitive 25; factors influencing potential 48; levels 48; questions surrounding 28

behaviour 10, 17, 32, 60, 75, 85; approach to understanding technology's impact 9; associated in coping research 74–5; bad 31; changing 74; digital age 32; exploring 4, 9; high-tech 21, 60; impact of technology 9, 16; motivated 52; and workplace stress 2–15

benefits 12, 19, 24, 30, 34, 39, 59, 79, 90; learning 21; positive 43; potential 59; workers 41

blood vessels 31, 87

boundaries 2–3, 10, 17, 53, 59, 72, 79; crossing 73; experiences of 39; international 30; merging 32; 'spanning' 7, 88; technology crossing 79

boundaryless workers 38

brain *see* human brain

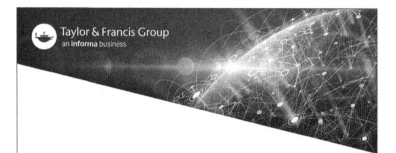

.

Printed in the United States
by Baker & Taylor Publisher Services